THE
MIGHTY
CHICKPEA

THE MIGHTY CHICKPEA

OVER 65 VEGETARIAN & VEGAN RECIPES

RYLAND PETERS & SMALL
LONDON • NEW YORK

Designer Paul Stradling
Editor Emily Calder
Head of Production Patricia Harrington
Art Director Leslie Harrington
Editorial Director Julia Charles
Publisher Cindy Richards
Proofreader Gillian Haslam
Indexer Hilary Bird

First published in 2022 by Ryland Peters & Small
20–21 Jockey's Fields
London WC1R 4BW
and
341 E 116th St
New York, NY 10029

www.rylandpeters.com

10 9 8 7 6 5 4 3 2 1

Recipe collection compiled by Emily Calder
Text © Ghillie Başan, Jordan Bourke, Chloe Coker
& Jane Montgomery, Ross Dobson, Ursula Ferrigno,
Amy Ruth Finegold, Mat Follas, Liz Franklin, Nicola
Graimes, Dunja Gulin, Jenny Linford, Vicky Jones,
Jackie Kearney, Theo A. Michaels, Hannah Miles,
Nitisha Patel, Claire Power, Milli Taylor, Jenny
Tschiesche, Leah Vanderveldt, Laura Washburn,
Sarah Wilkinson, Jenna Zoe 2022.

Design and photographs © Ryland Peters & Small
2022 (see page 144 for photo credits).

ISBN: 978-1-78879-425-1

A CIP record for this book is available from the
British Library.
US Library of Congress Cataloging-in-Publication
Data has been applied for.

Printed and bound in China.

NOTES

• **To cook your own chickpeas:** before cooking, soak the dried chickpeas in water for 12 hours – 170 g/1 cup chickpeas requires 2 litres/8 cups soaking water. Drain, place in a heavy-based pan and cover completely with fresh water. Bring to the boil over a high heat, uncovered. Using a slotted spoon, remove any foam that might appear. Lower the heat, cover and cook until tender – usually 1 hour or more. Check every 20 minutes and add more hot water if needed.

• Feel free to use canned chickpeas if you do not have time to cook them. Keep in mind that 170 g/1 cup dried chickpeas yields approx 345 g/2½ cups when cooked.

• Some countries refer to chickpeas as garbanzo beans. For the purposes of this book, they are referred to as chickpeas.

• Both British (metric) and American (imperial plus US cups) are included in these recipes for your convenience; however it is important to work with one set of measurements and not alternate between the two within a recipe.

• All spoon measurements are level unless otherwise specified.

• All eggs are medium (UK) or large (US), unless otherwise specified. Uncooked or partially cooked eggs should not be served to the very old, frail, young children, pregnant women or those with compromised immune systems.

• When a recipe calls for the grated zest of citrus fruit, buy unwaxed fruit and wash well before using. If you can only find treated fruit, scrub well in warm soapy water before using.

• Ovens should be preheated to the specified temperatures. We recommend using an oven thermometer. If using a fan-assisted oven, adjust temperatures according to the manufacturer's instructions.

CONTENTS

INTRODUCTION

A prince among pulses, the humble chickpea is a versatile and nutritious staple to vegan and vegetarian diets and beyond. Anyone seeking a fix of fibre, iron and slow-release energy need only look to the protein-packed chickpea. Chickpeas are an affordable and versatile legume, with their neutral taste promising an easy pairing with both sweet and savoury ingredients. If you're seeking anything from a fool-proof Creamy Hummus recipe, to a vegan-friendly Aquafaba Pavlova, there has never been a better time to champion the chickpea.

Grown primarily in India, chickpeas are a staple most common in Indian, Mediterranean and Middle-Eastern dishes. The legume provides a versatile and filling texture to complement other flavours in a dish, making it a very useful addition to soups, stews and curries. This book provides everything from a quintessential Falafel Pitta Pocket to an Indian Chana Masala, but the versatility of the chickpea goes far beyond its classic uses. There are endless ways to make the most of this tasty pulse, so try the recipes for Vegan Devilled 'Eggs', Chickpea 'Chuna' Quesadillas and Hummus & Walnut Crêpes.

The Mighty Chickpea features over 65 creative recipes for everything from comforting snacks to nutritious sheet pans and hearty soups. This book has a recipe for every occasion. For dinner parties and summer barbecues, those who love to host may opt for Hot Hummus with Pine Nuts & Chilli Butter, or Beetroot, Dill & Goat's Cheese Cups. Those seeking a nutritious and tasty lunch can turn to Perfectly Charred Falafel Burgers, Avocado & Chickpea Wraps, or a Chickpea, Tomato & Green Bean Minestrone Soup. For cosy winter evenings, or indeed dinners in any season, the Spicy Carrot & Chickpea Tagine, Moroccan Pumpkin Stew and Vegan Baked Chickpea Fajitas offer yet another way of utilising the power of the pulse. Finally, for those keen to inject more nutrition into their sweet-toothed moments, why not try the tempting Chickpea Fudge Cookies or Chocolate Chickpea Dip?

1

DIPS, SNACKS & SMALL BITES

CREAMY HUMMUS

This perfect recipe will be the base for other recipes in this book. Do cook your own chickpeas according to the instructions on page 4. Canned chickpeas can be used too (in this case, just use the cooking water from the can), but keep in mind that the deliciousness of the hummus made with freshly cooked, lukewarm chickpeas puts the bland-tasting versions made with canned chickpeas to shame!

320 g/2¼ cups cooked
  chickpeas (see page 4),
  plus 60 ml/¼ cup
  of the cooking liquid,
  or more if needed, plus
  2 tablespoons cooked
  chickpeas to serve
2 tablespoons extra-virgin
  olive oil, plus extra
  to serve
1 tablespoon tahini
3 garlic cloves
freshly squeezed juice of
  ½ a lemon, or to taste
½ teaspoon salt, or to taste
freshly chopped flat-leaf
  parsley, to garnish
  (optional)

SERVES 2-4

Blend all the ingredients in a blender or food processor, except the extra chickpeas and olive oil to serve, slowly adding the cooking liquid until you reach a thick and creamy consistency; this will take about 1 minute. High-speed blenders make the creamiest texture and need less liquid and time, but both food processors and stick blenders can be used as well. Adjust the lemon juice and salt to taste.

Serve topped with about 2 tablespoons extra-virgin olive oil and 2 tablespoons whole chickpeas. Garnish with chopped flat-leaf parsley, if you like.

BROAD BEAN HUMMUS

This is a fresh alternative to traditional hummus. The nutty flavour of broad/fava beans works really well with lemon and the sesame of the tahini.

300 g/2¼ cups fresh broad/ fava beans
400-g/14-oz. can chickpeas, drained and rinsed
50 g/¼ cup tahini
2 roasted garlic cloves (see Note)
grated zest and freshly squeezed juice of 1 lemon
salt and freshly ground black pepper, to season
toasted bread, to serve

SERVES 4

Put the broad/fava beans in a saucepan of cold, unsalted water and set over a medium heat. Bring to a low simmer and continue to simmer for 5 minutes. Drain, then put in a bowl of cold water and chill in the fridge to halt the cooking. After a few minutes, remove the outer skins and discard, reserving the inner beans to use in the hummus.

Put the beans and the remaining ingredients in a large mixing bowl with ½ teaspoon of salt. Blend to a fine paste using a handheld electric blender. Taste the mixture and add extra salt if needed. Sprinkle with black pepper and serve right away with toasted bread or cover and store in the fridge for up to 4 days.

Note: To roast garlic, place a whole bulb of garlic on a baking sheet and cook in a preheated oven at 180°C (350°F) Gas 4 for 45 minutes. You can easily do this while you're cooking something else and save it in the fridge until you need it. You will now have a bulb of soft garlic paste that can be squeezed, like a tube of toothpaste, one clove at a time.

PURPLE BEETROOT HUMMUS

The earthy intense sweetness of baked beets adds a deep, rich flavour
to this hummus.

2 beetroots/beets, well washed, with skin
1 quantity Creamy Hummus (see page 11)
1 teaspoon caraway seeds
salt, to season
olive oil, for drizzling

baking sheet lined with parchment paper

SERVES 2-4

Preheat the oven to 200°C (400°F) Gas 6.

Rub a pinch of salt into the beetroots/beets. Wrap them well in foil. Place on the lined baking sheet and bake in the preheated oven for about 45 minutes, or until the beetroot flesh is soft. Let cool slightly. Peel, discard the skins and tops and blend in a blender or food processor into a smooth purée.

Blend the beetroot purée into the creamy hummus a little at a time (reserving a little to swirl in at the end if, you like). It should be done slowly until the desired consistency, colour and taste are reached. Taste and adjust the seasoning. Stir through the caraway seeds or sprinkle on top. Swirl through any reserved beetroot purée and drizzle with extra olive oil to serve, if you like.

HOT HUMMUS WITH PINE NUTS & CHILLI BUTTER

When most people think of hummus, they think of the ubiquitous thick, smooth, chickpea purée served at room temperature with pitta bread or crudités, not this delectable, hot version, called *sicak* hummus in Turkish. This recipe is similar to the traditional recipe, but with the addition of yogurt, to make it more mousse-like and utterly moreish.

2 x 400-g/14-oz. cans chickpeas, drained and rinsed
2 teaspoons cumin seeds
2–3 garlic cloves, crushed
about 4 tablespoons olive oil
freshly squeezed juice of 2 lemons
2 tablespoons tahini
500 ml/2 cups thick, creamy yogurt
2 tablespoons pine nuts
50 g/3 tablespoons butter
1 teaspoon finely chopped dried red chilli/chile
sea salt and freshly ground black pepper, to season
warm crusty bread, to serve

SERVES 4-6

Preheat the oven to 200°C (400°F) Gas 6.

Instead of using a pestle and mortar to pound the chickpeas to a paste in the traditional manner, make life easy and tip the chickpeas into an electric blender. Add the cumin seeds, garlic, olive oil and lemon juice and whizz the mixture to a thick paste. Add the tahini and continue to blend until the mixture is really thick and smooth. Add the yogurt and whizz until the mixture has loosened a little and the texture is creamy. Season generously with salt and pepper and tip the mixture into an ovenproof dish.

Roast the pine nuts in small frying pan/skillet until they begin to brown and emit a nutty aroma. Add the butter to the pine nuts and stir until it melts. Stir in the chopped chilli/chile and pour the melted butter over the hummus, spooning the pine nuts all over the surface.

Pop the dish into the preheated oven for about 25 minutes, until the hummus has risen a little and most of the butter has been absorbed.

Serve immediately with chunks of warm crusty bread.

SOCCA CRACKERS *(pictured)*

These crackers are delicious, and a great source of protein. They make a lovely dipper for hummus and a range of other dips.

75 g/¾ cup chickpea/gram
   flour
1 tablespoon nutritional
   yeast
½ teaspoon sea salt
¼ teaspoon garlic powder
¼ teaspoon ground cumin

baking sheet lined with
   parchment paper

MAKES ABOUT 25 CRACKERS

Preheat the oven to 200°C (400°F) Gas 6.

In a bowl, combine all the ingredients together with 200 ml/1 cup water, using a whisk to remove any lumps. Pour the mixture onto the baking sheet, spreading it out in an even layer, and bake in the preheated oven for 25–30 minutes. After 20 minutes of cooking, take the socca flatbread out of the oven and slice it into crackers using a sharp knife before flipping them and placing them back onto the baking sheet. Return to the oven to crisp up for 5–10 minutes. Remove from the oven and leave to cool.

Store in an airtight container.

CUMIN-ROASTED CHICKPEAS

These make a fantastic topping to a meal or salad. They work really well with many of the Asian-inspired recipes in this book.

400-g/14-oz. can chickpeas,
   drained and rinsed
1 teaspoon garlic powder
1 teaspoon onion powder
½ teaspoon ground cumin
1 tablespoon olive oil
¼–½ teaspoon sea salt

SERVES 2

Preheat the oven to 200°C (400°F) Gas 6.

In a bowl, toss the chickpeas in the garlic powder, onion powder, cumin and olive oil.

Put the chickpeas on a baking sheet with sides. Bake in the preheated oven for 30 minutes until lightly toasted. Shake the pan a couple of times during the baking time to ensure the chickpeas cook evenly.

Remove from the oven. Sprinkle over the salt to taste. Serve hot or cold. If serving cold, allow to cool then store in an airtight container until ready to be consumed. They are best eaten within 24 hours.

LINSEED-SPECKLED HUMMUS WITH KALE CRISPS

This recipe is a double dose of linseed/flaxseed, and is a great source of omega 3s. Kale, baked in the oven with a cheesy seasoning, is delicious as a crisp for this!

400 g/3 cups cooked
    chickpeas (see page 4)
2 tablespoons tahini
freshly squeezed juice of
    2 large lemons
2 tablespoons water
2 garlic cloves, crushed
1 teaspoon ground cumin
1 tablespoon linseed/
    flaxseed oil
1 tablespoon milled
    linseeds/flaxseeds
sea salt and freshly ground
    black pepper, to taste

KALE CRISPS
1 medium head of curly kale
2 tablespoons olive oil
1 tablespoon Parmesan-style
    cheese or nutritional
    yeast flakes if you are
    dairy-free
1 teaspoon onion powder
    or 2 small chopped
    onions
½ teaspoon Himalayan
    salt

SERVES 4

For the hummus, blend all of the ingredients in a food processor and spoon into a serving bowl.

For the kale crisps, preheat the oven to 95°C (200°F) Gas ¼.

Wash and dry the kale. Mix the oil, Parmesan/nutritional yeast flakes, onion powder/chopped onion and salt in a bowl. Add the kale leaves to the bowl and coat with the oil mixture. Put the kale leaves on a baking sheet and cook in the preheated oven for 45 minutes. Keep an eye on them so as not to burn the edges.

Cool and serve with the hummus or store in an airtight container for up to 3 days.

VEGAN DEVILLED 'EGGS'

Vegan devilled 'eggs' are so tasty and a great way to use up left-over hummus! The skin on the potatoes should be just scrubbed instead of peeled, if possible. It adds a wonderful earthy aroma. Yummy!

480–600 g/6 egg-sized baby potatoes
1 tablespoon olive oil
160 g/1 cup left-over hummus
¼ teaspoon ground turmeric
½ teaspoon sweet or spicy smoked paprika, to serve
salt, to season
micro greens, to garnish

baking sheet lined with parchment paper

MAKES 12 PIECES

Preheat the oven to 200°C (400°F) Gas 6.

Scrub the potatoes well if using baby potatoes with delicate thin skins; otherwise peel them. Cut them in half lengthways and rub in the oil and a little salt. Place on the baking sheet cut sides up and bake in the preheated oven for 40–45 minutes or until golden and soft.

Meanwhile, place the hummus in a small saucepan and gently warm through, add the turmeric and mix well to incorporate.

When the potatoes are done, let them cool slightly, then spoon some of the potato flesh out of each half and add 1½ tablespoons of hummus to each. (Save the removed potato flesh for another recipe.)

Sprinkle with smoked paprika and serve, sprinkled with micro greens if you wish.

PARTY TARTLETS WITH HUMMUS

Think of these party tartlets as an elevated way to serve hummus and crackers. You can put single servings of a delicious dip into each tartlet and have them as a contained and neat party snack.

2 tablespoons ground linseeds/flaxseeds
6 tablespoons water
170 g/1½ cups ground almonds
a pinch of salt
2 tablespoons nutritional yeast
1½ teaspoons baking powder
dried oregano, to serve

HUMMUS FILLING
400-g/14-oz. can chickpeas, drained and rinsed
freshly squeezed juice of 1 lemon
2 tablespoons tahini
1 tablespoon olive oil
sea salt and freshly ground black pepper, to season

12 tartlet moulds

MAKES 12

Preheat the oven to 180°C (350°F) Gas 4.

Put the linseeds/flaxseeds and water in a small bowl. Whisk the seeds into the water with a fork until the mixture starts to feel like the consistency of a beaten egg. Place in the fridge.

Put the ground almonds, salt, nutritional yeast and baking powder in a food processor. Blitz together. At the last minute, add the 'flax egg' and blitz again but only it has been well incorporated – you don't want to overmix this. You should see a ball of dough start to form. Remove the dough from the processor and divide it into 12. Press each portion into a tartlet mould so that it neatly lines the base and sides of the mould. Trim off any excess dough with a sharp knife.

Put the tartlet moulds on a baking sheet in the middle of the preheated oven and bake for about 15 minutes, until you see the edges of the tartlets start to brown. Allow the tartlet cases to cool for a few minutes, at which point they should pop right out of the moulds.

For the hummus filling, blitz all the ingredients together in a food processor until smooth. Fill each tartlet case with a generous tablespoon of hummus and sprinkle a little oregano over the top.

BEETROOT, DILL & GOAT'S CHEESE CUPS

A tasty and nutritious bite, these cupped snacks are colourful and packed with flavour. The goat's cheese and dill garnish makes them even more pleasing to the eye.

400-g/14-oz. can chickpeas, drained and rinsed
250 g/9 oz. cooked beetroot/beets
1 large garlic clove
2 tablespoons olive oil
1 tablespoon freshly squeezed lemon juice
1½ tablespoons tahini
2–3 large pinches of salt
160 g/5½ oz. soft goat's cheese
fresh dill, to garnish

40 store-bought canapé cups

MAKES 40

Put the drained chickpeas, cooked beetroot/beets, garlic, olive oil, lemon juice, tahini and salt in a food processor, and blend until smooth.

Place a teaspoonful of the mixture in each canapé cup, and top with ½ teaspoon goat's cheese. Garnish with dill and serve.

CHICKPEA FLOUR & HARISSA PATTIES

If you're looking for an instant falafel recipe that does not require any prep work, check out these crunchy beauties! Serving them with a fair amount of sauce is key since the use of chickpea/gram flour, instead of soaked chickpeas, results in a somewhat drier consistency.

120 g/1 cup chickpea/gram flour
¼ teaspoon bicarbonate of soda/baking soda
½ teaspoon salt
½ teaspoon ground coriander
1 teaspoon harissa powder, or to taste
¼ teaspoon dried oregano
30 g/1 tablespoon very finely chopped onion
80 ml/⅓ cup hot water
3 tablespoons coconut oil or other, for frying
harissa paste, and Tofu Mayonnaise (see below) to serve (optional)

MAKES 8-10 PATTIES

TOFU MAYONNAISE
300 g/2 cups fresh tofu
600 ml/¼ cup olive or sunflower oil
3 tablespoons freshly squeezed lemon juice or apple cider vinegar
1 soft date
½ teaspoon salt

MAKES ABOUT 240 ML/1 CUP

First, make the Tofu Mayonnaise. Blend all the ingredients together with 6 tablespoons water until completely smooth. Taste and adjust the seasonings according to preference.

For the patties, combine the flour with other dry ingredients, mix in the chopped onion and slowly start incorporating the hot water. You should get a non-sticky dough that can easily be shaped. Set aside for 10 minutes before forming into small patties.

Heat the oil in a non-stick frying pan/skillet on a medium heat. Depending on the size of your pan you will need to fry them in at least two batches. Make sure not to overcrowd the pan! Lower the heat, add the patties and fry for 3–4 minutes on each side, or until golden brown.

If you wish to build your spicy food tolerance, serve with plenty of harissa paste, as well as tofu mayonnaise to cool!

CHICKPEA NUGGETS

Made with wholesome natural ingredients, this is a fun recipe. To make them gluten-free, use gluten-free oats and make the crumbs using quinoa flakes or gluten-free breadcrumbs. Store them in an airtight container and reheat in the oven or sandwich presser.

400-g/14-oz. can chickpeas, drained and rinsed
40 g/⅓ cup rolled/old-fashioned oats
2 tablespoons linseeds/flaxseeds
1–2 tablespoons oat milk
1 teaspoon onion powder
½ teaspoon garlic powder
½ teaspoon dried Italian herbs
a pinch of salt and freshly ground black pepper

CRUMBS
60 g/½ cup wholemeal/whole-wheat breadcrumbs or quinoa flakes
125 ml/½ cup oat milk

baking sheet lined with parchment paper

MAKES 15

Preheat the oven to 190°C (375°F) Gas 5.

Put the chickpeas into a food processor or high-speed blender. Add the oats, linseeds/flaxseeds, oat milk, onion and garlic powders, dried herbs and salt and pepper and pulse to blend until well combined and the chickpeas are finely chopped. Do not over blend.

For the outer crumbs, put the breadcrumbs or quinoa flakes and oat milk into 2 separate small bowls. Shape the chickpea dough into 15 even-size nuggets. Dip each nugget, one at a time, into the milk, then into the breadcrumbs, coating both sides and then put each one onto the prepared baking sheet.

Bake in the preheated oven for 10–15 minutes, turning halfway. Serve hot with fries, dips and sauces.

PAN-FRIED CHICKPEA FRITTERS

Simple and quick, these are perfect for a light lunch, or as a casual appetizer. You can also experiment a little, by adding in or substituting your favourite herbs or spices.

2 teaspoons cumin seeds
½ teaspoon dried chilli/
 hot red pepper flakes
250 g/1 cup soy or Greek
 yogurt
1 tablespoon pure maple
 syrup
120 g/1 cup spelt flour
 (white or wholegrain)
½ teaspoon baking powder
170 ml/¾ cup rice, soy or
 dairy milk
1 egg, lightly beaten
400-g/14-oz. can chickpeas,
 drained and rinsed
100 g/1 small red onion,
 finely chopped
a small handful of fresh
 flat-leaf parsley, finely
 chopped
a small handful of fresh
 coriander/cilantro, finely
 chopped
olive oil or vegetable oil,
 for frying
1 spring onion/scallion,
 finely sliced diagonally
sea salt and freshly ground
 black pepper, to season
extra virgin olive oil, for
 drizzling

MAKES 16

In a dry frying pan/skillet, gently fry the cumin seeds over a medium heat until aromatic. Pound ½ of them to a powder using a pestle and mortar, and keep the other ½ to one side. In a bowl, combine together the ground cumin, chilli/hot red pepper flakes, yogurt, maple syrup and a good pinch of sea salt. Set to one side.

Place the flour and baking powder in a large bowl, slowly whisk in the rice, soy or dairy milk and beaten egg, until well combined with no lumps. Add in the chickpeas, red onion, almost all of the herbs, remaining cumin seeds, ¾ teaspoon sea salt and a few grindings of black pepper. Stir together to combine.

Place 1 tablespoon of olive or vegetable oil in a large, non-stick frying pan/skillet and set over a medium-high heat. Once hot, add 2 level tablespoons of batter for each fritter and flatten into little rounds. Fry in batches, without overcrowding the pan, for about 5 minutes, turning once, until they are golden brown and cooked through.

To serve, pile the fritters up on individual plates and scatter over the sliced spring onion/scallion and extra parsley. Finally, drizzle over some extra virgin olive oil. Spoon the set-aside yogurt mixture over the top or serve it in a bowl on the side. Serve with a green salad.

CHICKPEA BITES

These reheat well so it's worth making a large batch to enjoy over a few days or for the freezer (defrost before reheating). Serve with brown rice and sliced raw vegetables: cucumbers, cherry tomatoes, carrots and celery. They are also good cold as a sandwich filler, with mayonnaise and some shredded lettuce.

1 small onion, coarsely chopped
1 carrot, coarsely chopped
1 celery stick/rib, coarsely chopped
1 garlic clove, peeled
2–3 tablespoons extra virgin olive oil or rapeseed/canola oil
400-g/14-oz. can chickpeas, drained and rinsed
2 generous tablespoons mayonnaise
2 tablespoons oatbran
1 tablespoon wholemeal/whole-wheat flour
freshly squeezed juice of ½ an orange
sea salt and freshly ground black pepper, to season
plain Greek yogurt, to serve (optional)

non-stick baking sheet, lightly greased

MAKES 12-15 BITES

Preheat the oven to 200°C (400°F) Gas 6.

Put the onion, carrot, celery and garlic in the bowl of a food processor and process until finely chopped.

Heat the oil in a small non-stick frying pan/skillet. When hot, add the vegetable mixture, season with salt and pepper and cook for 3–5 minutes, stirring often until soft. Do not allow the mixture to brown or the garlic will taste bitter. Let cool slightly.

Meanwhile, put the chickpeas, mayonnaise, oatbran, flour and orange juice into the same food processor bowl and process, leaving some small chunks of chickpea; the mixture should not be completely smooth. Transfer the chickpea mixture to a large bowl. Add the vegetable mixture and stir well. Taste and adjust the seasoning.

Form the mixture into walnut-size balls and arrange on the prepared baking sheet. Bake in the preheated oven for 30–40 minutes, until brown and just golden on top. Serve hot, warm or at room temperature.

DHOKLA MUFFINS

These traditional Gujarati snacks are savoury steamed muffins made from chickpea/gram flour. Because the savoury, light, fluffy cake is steamed, it is healthy and nutritious, as well as packing a flavour punch.

50 g/¼ cup caster/
  granulated sugar

BATTER
190 g/1¼ cups semolina
25 g/¼ cup chickpea/gram
  flour
230 g/generous 1 cup
  natural/plain yogurt
½ teaspoon finely grated
  garlic
1 teaspoon finely grated
  fresh root ginger
1 teaspoon chopped green
  chilli/chile
1 teaspoon caster/
  granulated sugar
1 teaspoon salt
150 ml/⅔ cup warm water
1½ teaspoons fruit salt

SEASONED OIL
3 tablespoons vegetable oil
1 teaspoon mustard seeds
1 teaspoon sesame seeds

TO SERVE
freshly chopped coriander/
  cilantro
unsweetened desiccated/
  dried shredded coconut
chutney or dipping sauce

steamer (optional)
8 muffin moulds, greased
  and lined with parchment
  paper

MAKES 8

Combine all of the ingredients for the batter together apart from the fruit salt. Cover the batter and leave for 10 minutes to rest and ferment.

Meanwhile, set up your steamer. If you do not have a steamer, you can pour boiling water into a large saucepan and insert a stand for the moulds to sit on (the moulds should not touch the water directly). At this point you need to ensure that the steamer is absolutely ready, because once you put the fruit salt into the fermented batter, you need to cook the muffins straight away for the best texture. Set the muffin moulds out ready for use. If you do not have metal muffin moulds, you can also use ramekins.

Once you are all set up, quickly add the fruit salt and 2 teaspoons of water to the batter and mix well. Quickly and evenly distribute the batter between the moulds. Put them into the steamer with a lid on and steam for 10–12 minutes. You can check whether the muffins are ready or not by poking the centre with a clean knife; if the knife comes out clean, then the muffins are fully cooked. They should be light and spongy. Remove the muffins from the steamer and set aside to cool.

Meanwhile, prepare a sugared water by heating the sugar and 200 ml/¾ cup of water together in a pan until the sugar completely dissolves. Set the pan aside and leave to cool slightly.

Take the muffins out of the moulds and put on a wire rack, gently prick with a cocktail stick/toothpick and pour a little sugared water over each muffin, no more than a tablespoonful on each.

Next, make the seasoned oil. Heat the oil in a frying pan/skillet over a medium heat, add mustard seeds and allow to sizzle and pop. Add sesame seeds, mix well for 10 seconds and remove from the heat. Spoon a little of the oil and seed mix onto each muffin. Garnish with the chopped coriander/cilantro and coconut. Serve hot or cold, with your choice of chutney or dipping sauce.

CHICKPEA SOCCA PANCAKES WITH MUSHROOMS & THYME

Socca are crispy-edged Mediterranean pancakes made with chickpea/ gram flour. They are perfect for topping with savoury or sweet ingredients. Slightly thicker than crepes, socca have a nutty-sweet flavour and a high protein content which makes them more of a wholesome, filling meal. They can be eaten for a fancy-ish breakfast or a laid-back dinner with a big green salad on the side. In this recipe, socca is paired with earthy mushrooms, but you can play around with whatever fillings you'd like. These are also nice with roasted tomatoes and a fried egg, or coconut yogurt and sliced fruit.

125 g/1 cup chickpea/gram flour
½ teaspoon salt
olive oil or butter, for frying

MUSHROOMS
1 tablespoon olive oil or butter
5 sprigs of fresh thyme, leaves removed from the stems
225 g/8 oz. cremini mushrooms, sliced
1 garlic clove, finely minced or grated
salt and freshly ground black pepper, to season

OPTIONAL TOPPINGS
grated Parmesan-style or Gruyère cheese
a fried egg

SERVES 2

Put the chickpea/gram flour, salt and 295 ml/1¼ cups water into a large bowl and mix together with a whisk or a fork until well combined into a smooth batter. Leave to stand at room temperature for at least 10 minutes.

Meanwhile, heat a thin layer of oil or butter in a large frying pan/ skillet over a high heat. Add the thyme leaves and mushrooms and cook, stirring occasionally, for 2–3 minutes until the mushrooms soften and are slightly golden. Reduce the heat to medium, then add the garlic and cook for 1 minute more. Season to taste with salt and pepper. Keep the mushrooms warm in a low oven or in a covered dish while you cook the pancakes.

Heat the olive oil or butter in another small frying pan/skillet over a medium heat. Add approximately 60–75 ml/¼–scant ⅓ cup of the socca batter to the warm pan. Swirl it around so that it covers the base of the pan. Fry for about 2–3 minutes, until the batter begins to form bubbles. Flip the pancake with a spatula and cook for another 1–2 minutes on the other side.

Repeat with the remaining batter. This should make you about 4 small socca pancakes in total. Serve with the mushrooms and any additional toppings you like.

HERBY CHICKPEA PANCAKES WITH HALLOUMI & ROASTED CORN & RED PEPPER SALSA

Serve these tasty, gluten-free pancakes for a substantial weekend brunch or as a light lunch or supper. The crunchy salsa can be made ahead of time.

130 g/1 cup chickpea/gram flour
1 teaspoon salt
½ teaspoon ground cumin
¼ teaspoon ground turmeric
½ x 400-g/14-oz. can chickpeas, drained, rinsed and crushed
240 ml/1 cup milk
1 egg
1 garlic clove, crushed
freshly grated zest and juice of 1 lemon
a handful of freshly chopped herbs
1 teaspoon bicarbonate of soda/baking soda
250 g/9 oz. halloumi, sliced
1 tablespoon olive oil

ROASTED CORN & RED PEPPER SALSA
2 sweet red (bell) peppers, halved
2 sweetcorn cobs
a handful of cherry tomatoes
3 tablespoons olive oil
½ red onion, finely diced
½–1 fresh red chilli/chile, finely diced
a handful of fresh coriander/cilantro, finely chopped
freshly squeezed juice of ½ a lime
1 teaspoon white wine vinegar
1 teaspoon granulated sugar
salt and freshly ground black pepper, to season

SERVES 6-8

Preheat the oven to 200°C (400°F) Gas 6.

To make the salsa, put the peppers in a roasting pan skin-side up, with the sweetcorn cobs and tomatoes. Sprinkle well with salt and pepper and drizzle with 2 tablespoons olive oil. Roast in the top half of the preheated oven for 20–25 minutes. Reserve any juices left in the pan. Allow to cool slightly, then peel the skin off the peppers and remove the corn kernels from the cobs. Finely chop the peppers and break up the tomatoes with a fork, then put them in a bowl with the onion, chilli/chile and coriander/cilantro.

In a separate bowl, combine the lime juice, vinegar, sugar and remaining olive oil. Season with salt and pepper and stir until well combined. Pour over the vegetable mixture and stir.

To make the pancakes, put the chickpea/gram flour, salt, cumin and turmeric in a bowl. Stir in the crushed chickpeas. In a separate bowl, combine the milk, egg, garlic and lemon juice and zest and beat well with a fork until well combined. Make a well in the centre of the dry ingredients, pour in the milk mixture and stir from the centre until well combined. Add the chopped herbs, cover and set aside in the fridge for 20 minutes or until you are ready. Just before you make the pancakes, stir in the bicarbonate of soda/baking soda.

Lightly grease a frying pan/skillet and set over a medium–high heat. Add a ladle of batter and cook until bubbles begin to form and the pancake starts to firm up. Turn it over and cook until both sides are golden brown and it has puffed up slightly.

Lightly oil the halloumi and cook over a high heat on a stovetop griddle/grill pan for 1 minute on each side. Put the pancakes onto serving plates, top with halloumi and salsa and serve.

CHICKPEA 'OMELETTES'

These chickpea 'omelettes' or crêpes are great for lunch filled with vegetables, mushrooms, baby spinach or cheese. They are highly nutritious and packed with plant-based protein. They are very convenient to make and also really easy. They can be a great savoury breakfast, with their high protein content setting you up for a healthy start to the day. This is a great way to make an omelette without using eggs.

80 g/⅔ cup chickpea/gram flour
2 tablespoons nutritional yeast
a pinch of ground turmeric
a pinch of salt
50 g/1 cup cooked chopped chard
75 g/1 cup sautéed sliced mushrooms
olive oil, for frying

SERVES 2

In a small bowl, whisk together the flour, nutritional yeast and turmeric with 180 ml/⅔ cup water until all the lumps have gone.

Heat a small frying pan/skillet over a medium heat and grease with olive oil. Pour half of the batter evenly into the pan and cook over a medium heat for a few minutes before flipping it and cooking the other side for a few minutes. Add half the chopped chard and sautéed mushrooms before folding the pancake in half and transferring to a plate. Cook the second omelette following the same method.

Variations: Add any of the following: ground cumin, crushed garlic, vegan or vegetarian cheese, diced avocado and your choice of vegetables and greens.

BAKED CHICKPEA PANCAKE

Known as *cecina* in Italy, this baked chickpea pancake makes a nice breakfast or light lunch, especially when served with a glass of chilled yogurt or kefir. It can also be cut into pieces and served as an appetizer with dips, salads or stews – it's a very versatile and tasty gluten-free and protein-rich pancake.

120 g/¾ cup chickpea/gram flour
360 ml/1½ cups yogurt or kefir whey
2 tablespoons olive oil
salt and freshly ground black pepper, to season

26–28 cm/10–11 in. cast iron pancake pan

SERVES 2

Whisk together the flour and yogurt or kefir whey, cover and let ferment for 6–10 hours.

Preheat the oven to 200°C (400°F) Gas 6.

Season the batter with salt and pepper. Using a silicone brush, oil the pan with one tablespoon of olive oil. Heat the pan in the oven, carefully take out and pour in the cecina batter. Add the remaining tablespoon of oil on top of the batter and gently whisk with a fork. Put the pan back in the oven and bake for 22–25 minutes.

Cecina should have a thin, crispy outside and a softer, creamy inside when done. Grill/broil for the last 3 minutes to form the crust, if necessary. Flip out of the pan, slice and serve hot, warm or cold.

SICILIAN CHICKPEA FRITTERS

In Sicily, chickpea/gram flour is boiled with water to make a thick batter, allowed to cool, then cut into squares and fried into irresistible soft-yet-crunchy fritters called *panelle*. Best eaten hot, they are often served in a sesame bun, like a burger.

250 g/2 cups chickpea/gram flour, sifted
1 teaspoon salt
1 tablespoon freshly chopped flat-leaf parsley
3 tablespoons olive oil
coarse sea salt and freshly ground black pepper, to season

30 x 20-cm/12 x 8-in. baking sheet, oiled

SERVES 4-6

Whisk the chickpea/gram flour into 1 litre/quart of water until there are no lumps, then season with the salt.

Heat the batter gently in a saucepan, stirring constantly, until it boils and thickens. Simmer the mixture for about 15 minutes, whisking constantly, as lumps tend to form otherwise. Stir in the parsley and cook for another 5 minutes.

Pour into the prepared baking sheet, and smooth out the surface. The mixture should be no more than 1 cm/⅜ in. thick. Leave to cool for several hours to allow the mixture to solidify.

Preheat the oven to 200°C (400°F) Gas 6.

When the batter has cooled and solidified, cut into triangles, squares or, to make chunky chips, batons about the size of your largest finger.

When the oven is hot, pour the olive oil onto a clean baking sheet and heat in the oven for a few minutes, then using a spatula, transfer the triangles, squares or batons to the hot oil, flipping over once to coat both sides with oil. Fry in the oven for about 20 minutes, until the panelle are crisp on the surface and starting to brown, then turn over and cook for another 10 minutes.

Alternatively, heat some oil in a frying pan/skillet, and fry the panelle on the hob/stovetop.

Sprinkle with coarse sea salt and black pepper and serve immediately, either as a snack with drinks or with a salad.

SPICED CHICKPEA & SPINACH PASTIES

These little turnover pasties make ideal food for nibbling with drinks, or for taking on picnics. The filling is Middle Eastern in character, while the soft pastry dough is more likely to be found in Georgia.

PASTRY
175 g/1⅓ cups all-purpose flour
½ teaspoon salt
75 g/⅓ cup butter, diced
2 eggs, beaten separately
5 tablespoons sour cream
1 tablespoon sesame seeds

CHICKPEA FILLING
250 g/1¼ cups cooked chickpeas (see page 4) or a 400-g/14-oz. can, drained and rinsed
2 tablespoons tahini
1 teaspoon ground cumin
1 teaspoon ground coriander
200 g/7 oz. spinach, cooked, squeezed dry and chopped
1 tablespoon freshly squeezed lemon juice
3 tablespoons olive oil
1 tablespoon freshly chopped flat-leaf parsley
2 tablespoons freshly chopped mint
1 tablespoon za'tar Middle Eastern spice mixture, or 1 tablespoon mixed dried oregano and thyme
salt and freshly ground black pepper, to season

MAKES ABOUT 20 PASTIES

Sift the flour and salt into a bowl and, using your fingers, rub in the diced butter until the mixture resembles fine breadcrumbs. Alternatively, put the flour and butter into a food processor and pulse for a few seconds. Add one of the beaten eggs and the sour cream and continue to mix until the dough starts to form a ball, then stop immediately.

Wrap the dough in a plastic bag and chill in the fridge for 20 minutes or until needed.

Meanwhile, make the filling. In the food processor, pulse the chickpeas to a rough purée, together with the tahini and the ground spices. Stir (don't purée) in the chopped spinach, lemon juice, olive oil, fresh herbs and za'tar, then season with a teaspoon of salt and some pepper.

Preheat the oven to 200°C/400°F/Gas 6.

Roll out the pastry thinly and cut circles about 9 cm/3½ in. in diameter. Place a spoonful of the chickpea mixture on each circle, brush the perimeter with the other beaten egg and fold over to make a little pasty. Place on a greased baking sheet, then repeat until all of the pastry has been used. Brush the surface of each pasty with beaten egg, sprinkle with sesame seeds and bake in the preheated oven for 15–20 minutes until golden.

FRIED CHICKPEAS WITH HERBS

This very simple Sicilian treatment of chickpeas is a popular street food, often eaten as a *merenda* or afternoon snack, and also commonly served at *Sagre* – festivals to celebrate the season of a particular ingredient. It's a welcome change from peanuts as an aperitivo, but also works in a salad.

200 g/1 cup plus
   2 tablespoons dried
   chickpeas, soaked in
   water overnight with
   2 bay leaves, 2 garlic
   cloves and a handful
   of fresh parsley
olive oil or groundnut oil,
   for frying
a handful of fresh rosemary
   needles
a handful of fresh sage
   leaves, finely chopped
a handful of fresh oregano
   leaves, finely chopped
1½ teaspoons fennel seeds
crushed sea salt, for
   sprinkling
finely grated zest of 1 lemon

SERVES 8

Drain the chickpeas and discard the soaking water, but keep the garlic and bay leaves.

Add the chickpeas, garlic and bay leaves to a saucepan filled with cold water. Cook according to the instructions on page 4. Strain and place on a dry, clean dish towel and pat to remove excess moisture.

Heat the oil in a large frying pan/skillet set over a medium heat and add a quarter of the chickpeas. Shallow-fry for 5 minutes. Add a quarter of the herbs and a quarter of the fennel seeds and cook for 3 minutes until fragrant. Remove with a slotted spoon and drain on paper towels. Repeat with the remaining ingredients in batches.

Transfer to a bowl and add sea salt to taste. Mix well and serve sprinkled with the zest of the lemon.

SPICY CHICKPEAS & ONIONS WITH YOGURT & PITTA BREAD

This dish of chickpeas on toasted pitta breads is a great street-food favourite and can be enjoyed at any time of the day.

250 g/1½ cups dried
  chickpeas, soaked in
  water overnight
2 bay leaves
3–4 black peppercorns
3–4 pitta breads
1 large red onion, cut into
  bite-sized slices
2–3 tablespoons olive oil
freshly squeezed juice of
  1 lemon
2 garlic cloves, crushed
1–2 teaspoons cumin seeds,
  roasted and lightly
  crushed
1–2 teaspoons paprika, or
  finely chopped dried
  chilli/chile
1–2 teaspoons dried mint
  (reserve a little to
  garnish)
2 tablespoons pine nuts
2 tablespoons samna (ghee),
  or butter

YOGURT
600 ml/2½ cups thick,
  creamy yogurt
2–3 garlic cloves, crushed
sea salt and freshly ground
  black pepper, to season

SERVES 4

Drain the chickpeas and tip them into a large saucepan. Cover with plenty of water and bring it to the boil. Add the bay leaves and peppercorns, and cook according to the instructions on page 4.

Meanwhile, beat the yogurt with the garlic in a bowl and season it with salt and pepper. Toast the pitta breads, break them up into bite-sized pieces and arrange them on a serving dish.

Drain the chickpeas and reserve roughly 4 tablespoons of the cooking liquid. While still hot, tip the chickpeas into a bowl and add the onion, olive oil, lemon juice, garlic, cumin seeds, paprika and dried mint.

Moisten the pitta breads with the reserved cooking liquid, place in a serving dish and spread the chickpeas over them. Spoon the yogurt over the top and sprinkle with the reserved dried mint.

Roast the pine nuts in a frying pan/skillet until they turn golden brown and emit a nutty aroma. Add the samna and, as soon as it melts, pour the mixture over the yogurt. Serve immediately, while the chickpeas are still warm.

2

SOUPS, SANDWICHES & SALADS

CHICKPEA & VEGETABLE SOUP WITH FETA

Often used as a substitute for potatoes, rice or meat, chickpeas are a great favourite in hearty stews and soups, such as this vegetarian version of the Moroccan lamb and chickpea *harira*, variations of which can be found throughout the Islamic world.

2–3 tablespoons olive oil
2 onions, chopped
2 celery sticks/ribs, trimmed and diced
2 small carrots, peeled and diced
2–3 garlic cloves, smashed
2 teaspoons cumin seeds
2 teaspoons coriander seeds
2–3 teaspoons ground turmeric
2 teaspoons sugar
2–3 bay leaves
2–3 whole dried chillies/chiles
1 tablespoon tomato purée/paste
1 litre/1¾ pints/4 cups vegetable stock or water
400-g/14-oz. can chopped tomatoes, drained of juice
400-g/14-oz. can chickpeas, drained and rinsed
sea salt and freshly ground black pepper, to season
a small bunch of fresh flat-leaf parsley, coarsely chopped
a small bunch of fresh coriander/cilantro, coarsely chopped
150 g/5½ oz. feta cheese, rinsed and drained
1 lemon, cut into quarters, to serve

SERVES 4–6

Heat the oil in the base of a deep, heavy-based saucepan. Stir in the onions, celery and carrots and cook until the onions begin to colour. Add the smashed garlic, cumin and coriander seeds and stir in the turmeric, sugar, bay leaves and chillies/chiles. Add the tomato purée/paste, pour in the stock and bring the liquid to the boil. Reduce the heat, cover with a lid and simmer for 10–15 minutes.

Add the chopped tomatoes and chickpeas and simmer for a further 10 minutes. Season the soup with salt and pepper and toss in most of the parsley and coriander/cilantro. Crumble the feta cheese over the top, sprinkle with the remaining herbs, and serve the soup with wedges of lemon to squeeze over it.

MOROCCAN CHICKPEA SOUP WITH FALAFEL & HARISSA POCKETS

Moroccan food is so flavoursome with hints of cinnamon and citrus as well as fiery heat. This recipe uses a harissa made with rose petals but if you cannot find it, substitute regular harissa paste instead.

3 shallots, finely chopped
15 g/1 tablespoon butter
1 tablespoon olive oil
1 garlic clove, finely sliced
1 teaspoon black onion/
    nigella seeds
1 teaspoon ground
    cinnamon
freshly squeezed juice of
    2 lemons
1 teaspoon rose harissa
2 x 400-g/14-oz. cans
    chickpeas, drained and
    rinsed
80 g/½ cup soft dried
    apricots
1 litre/quart vegetable stock
freshly ground black
    pepper, to season
fennel fronds, to garnish
    (optional)

FALAFEL POCKETS
1 teaspoon rose harissa
200 g/1 cup Greek yogurt
12 ready-made falafels
    (or see pages 65 or 74
    to make your own)
4 wholemeal pitta pockets
a few handfuls of mixed soft
    salad leaves
salt and freshly ground
    black pepper, to season

SERVES 4

For the soup, fry the shallots in the butter and olive oil until they are soft and translucent. Add the garlic and fry until lightly golden brown. Add the black onion/nigella seeds and cinnamon and fry for a minute to heat the spices, stirring all the time. Add the lemon juice, harissa, chickpeas, apricots and stock to the pan and simmer for about 20 minutes. Pour the soup into a blender or food processor and blitz until smooth. Return to the pan and keep warm.

To make the harissa yogurt dressing for the falafel pockets, fold the harissa into the Greek yogurt, season with salt and pepper to your taste, cover and store in the fridge until you are ready to serve.

When ready to serve, preheat the oven to the temperature recommended on the falafel packaging and cook the falafel following the package instructions. Warm the pitta breads under the grill/broiler and then cut them open. Fill each with salad leaves and falafel and top with a drizzle of the harissa yogurt dressing.

Pour the soup into bowls and top with chopped fennel fronds, if using, and freshly ground black pepper. Serve straight away with the falafel pockets on the side.

CHICKPEA, TOMATO & GREEN BEAN MINESTRONE SOUP

Often thought of as cold weather fare, this version has summer written all over it, and is packed with fresh tomatoes and green beans as well as chickpeas. This recipe has a few handfuls of rocket/arugula, to add more of a summery vibe. Its peppery bite lightens the soup, while making it much more than just another minestrone.

1 tablespoon olive oil
1 onion, chopped
2 garlic cloves, chopped
400-g/14-oz. can chickpeas, drained and rinsed
100 g/4 oz. green beans, sliced on the angle
6 ripe tomatoes, halved
a handful of freshly chopped flat-leaf parsley
1.5 litres/6 cups vegetable stock
100 g/3½ oz. wholemeal/ whole-wheat spaghetti, broken into 3–4-cm/ 2-in. pieces
2 handfuls of wild rocket/ arugula
50 g/1 cup finely grated Pecorino Romano or Parmesan-style cheese
sea salt and freshly ground black pepper, to season
crusty bread, to serve

SERVES 4

Put the oil in a large saucepan set over a medium heat. Add the onion, partially cover with a lid and cook for 4–5 minutes, stirring often, until softened. Add the garlic and cook for 1 minute. Add the chickpeas, green beans, tomatoes, parsley, stock and spaghetti and bring to the boil.

Reduce the heat and let simmer for 40 minutes, stirring often, until the pasta is cooked and the soup is thick. Season to taste with salt and pepper.

Just before serving, add the rocket/arugula and gently stir until it softens. Ladle the soup into warmed serving bowls and sprinkle a generous amount of grated cheese over the top. Serve immediately with chunks of crusty bread.

Next time: Try making this delicious soup with different vegetables. Courgettes/zucchini and carrots are a nice addition but remember that both take a little longer to cook so dice them very finely before adding to the soup with the other vegetables. A pinch of smoky Spanish paprika (pimentón) will add a slightly different flavour.

PASTA E FAGIOLI

This hearty soup of pasta and beans is a classic from the Puglia region of Italy. In this version of the recipe, beans are replaced with creamy chickpeas. The pasta shapes traditionally used are orecchiette, meaning 'little ears' but any small shape will work just as well.

250 g/1½ cups dried chickpeas
2 tablespoons olive oil
1 onion, finely chopped
2 garlic cloves, finely chopped
a sprig of fresh rosemary
¼ teaspoon dried chilli/hot red pepper flakes
400-g/14-oz. can chopped tomatoes
1 tablespoon tomato purée/paste
1.5 litres/6 cups vegetable stock
100 g/⅔ cup small pasta shapes such as orecchiette or conchigliette
sea salt and freshly ground black pepper, to season

TO SERVE
freshly grated Parmesan-style cheese
extra virgin olive oil

SERVES 4

Soak the chickpeas in cold water overnight. Drain and put in a large saucepan with sufficient cold water to cover. Bring to the boil, reduce the heat to medium and cook, uncovered, for 45 minutes, until very tender. Drain and set aside.

Heat the oil in a large, heavy-based saucepan set over a medium heat. Add the onion, garlic, rosemary and chilli/hot red pepper flakes along with a pinch of salt and cook for 8–10 minutes, stirring often, until the onion has softened.

Increase the heat to high. Stir in the tomatoes, tomato purée/paste, stock and the chickpeas and bring to the boil. Add the pasta, reduce the heat to a medium simmer and cook for about 20 minutes, until the pasta is tender. Season to taste with salt and pepper.

Serve sprinkled with Parmesan-style cheese and drizzled with olive oil.

FENNEL & LEMON-SCENTED FALAFEL POCKETS

This is a falafel recipe with a slightly different spice twist! The fennel taste from the seeds and the bulb itself pair well with the refreshing citrus.

180 g/1 cup dried chickpeas
2 shallots
2 garlic cloves
½ bunch of fresh fennel
   fronds or coriander/
   cilantro leaves
1 teaspoon fennel seeds,
   crushed
1 teaspoon grated lemon
   zest
½ teaspoon bicarbonate
   of soda/baking soda
1 teaspoon ground
   coriander
⅛ teaspoon chilli/chili
   powder
1½ teaspoons salt
230 ml/1 cup oil, for frying

TO SERVE
pitta pockets
Romaine lettuce leaves
fennel bulb, shaved into
   thin shavings using
   a vegetable peeler
pickles
tahini sauce
lemon wedges

MAKES 24–26 SMALL FALAFELS

Soak the chickpeas in plenty of water overnight.

It's best to use a food processor fitted with an 'S' blade for blending the falafel mix, even though it can also be done in a good blender, in two batches.

First blend the drained chickpeas; the texture should resemble coarse sand. Add all the remaining ingredients (except the frying oil) and blend until you get a paste. Cover with clingfilm/plastic wrap and let sit in the fridge for 1 hour, or longer.

Roll the falafel mixture into walnut-sized balls, wetting your hands once in a while to prevent sticking. Deep-fry the falafels in hot oil for 4 minutes or until nicely browned. Because we're using soaked chickpeas, these falafels need to be deep-fried to make them digestible – baking them wouldn't work.

Warm the pitta pockets and fill them with lettuce, fennel shavings, pickles and falafel balls and serve with tahini sauce and lemon wedges.

PERFECTLY CHARRED FALAFEL BURGERS

There's nothing quite like biting into a big, juicy falafel burger! A cast-iron pan/skillet is essential for frying these – it means they need very little oil but won't stick to the pan. It also uniquely gives the delicious charred flavour.

250 g/1½ cups cooked chickpeas (see page 4), well drained
130 g/¾ cup very finely grated beetroot/beets
130 g/1 cup pre-soaked couscous (pour 120 ml/ ½ cup boiling water over 65 g/½ cup couscous, add a little salt, cover and let sit for 10 minutes)
70 g/½ cup good-quality breadcrumbs
2 tablespoons tahini
3 tablespoons finely chopped onion
2 garlic cloves, crushed
¾ teaspoon salt
½ teaspoon dried thyme
½ teaspoon dried oregano
freshly ground black pepper
sunflower or coconut oil, for frying

TO SERVE
6 whole-wheat burger buns
lettuce leaves
Tofu Mayonnaise (see page 28)
slices of fresh onion
pickles
salsa

wooden barbecue sticks

SERVES 6

In a food processor fitted with an 'S' blade, pulse the chickpeas. Transfer to a mixing bowl and add all the remaining ingredients, except the frying oil. Use your hands to knead the mixture thoroughly; everything should be well incorporated. Chill in the fridge for 20 minutes, or longer.

Form the mixture into 6 patties. You can use a big cookie cutter or an American ½ cup measuring cup for 1 burger – lightly oil the inside to prevent sticking, fill the cup and turn it over onto a baking sheet. Pat down to make a nicely shaped burger.

Preheat a cast-iron pan/skillet over a medium heat. Pour in 1 tablespoon of oil and add 2–3 burgers (more if your pan is bigger). Fry for about 5 minutes each side, adding a tablespoon more oil after the flip. Cook until the burgers are heated through, slightly charred and have a thin crust.

Serving Suggestion: While the pan is still hot, fry the inside of a whole-wheat bun, spread the bottom part with your favourite burger-friendly condiment, add lettuce leaves, top with the burger, spread tofu mayo on top, add slices of fresh onion and top with the bun. Pierce with a wooden barbecue stick and add a couple of pickles. Best served with a salsa of your choosing!

SPICED LENTIL & CHICKPEA BURGERS

Here the iconic Mumbai street food classic, *Pau Bhaji*, is given a western twist. The traditional spiced vegetable mix is formed into a patty, with chickpeas and masoor dhal coming together to take centre stage.

2 Maris Piper or Yukon Gold potatoes, peeled and chopped into small chunks
400-g/14-oz. can chickpeas, drained and rinsed
250 g/9 oz. chestnut mushrooms
2 garlic cloves, peeled
50 g/1¾ oz. masoor dhal, picked and rinsed, then soaked in 100 ml/⅓ cup plus 1 tablespoon boiling water for 30 minutes, then drained
40 g/1 cup panko breadcrumbs
3 tablespoons vegetable oil
½ teaspoon cumin seeds
½ teaspoon dried chilli/hot red pepper flakes
¼ teaspoon ground turmeric
¼ teaspoon ground cumin
¼ teaspoon ground coriander
¼ teaspoon chaat masala
fine sea salt and freshly ground black pepper, to season
plain/all-purpose flour, for dredging the burgers
vegetable oil, for frying

TO SERVE
sliced Little Gem/Bibb lettuce
sliced beef tomato
sliced red onion
6 burger buns, sliced in half
Indian pickle

baking sheet, lined with parchment paper

SERVES 6

Cook the potatoes in a large saucepan of boiling water for 12–15 minutes until soft and mashable.

Meanwhile, place the chickpeas in a food processor and pulse until they are coarsely chopped. Remove and set aside. Place the mushrooms and garlic in the food processor and pulse until coarsely chopped. Remove and set aside.

Drain the potatoes and mash them well. In a mixing bowl, combine the potatoes with the mushrooms and garlic, the chickpeas, soaked and drained lentils, panko breadcrumbs, vegetable oil, cumin seeds, chilli/hot red pepper flakes, turmeric, cumin, coriander and chaat masala. Season generously with salt and pepper and mix to evenly combine.

Use your hands to scoop out 6 equal portions of the mixture (about 150 g/5¼ oz. each), and mould them into patty shapes. Space the patties out evenly on a tray and chill in the fridge for around 15 minutes.

Preheat the oven to 180°C (350°F) Gas 4.

Spread some flour out on a plate and dredge the chilled patties in the flour, turning them to coat all over.

Put the oil into a frying pan/skillet and, when hot, add the patties. Fry on each side for about 2 minutes until golden brown. As they are frying, gently spoon over some of the hot oil to seal the sides of the patties.

Transfer the fried patties to the prepared baking sheet and bake in the preheated oven for 12–15 minutes to cook all the way through.

To build the burgers, place some lettuce, sliced tomato and onion on the bottom half of each bun, followed by a cooked patty. Sandwich on the bun lids and serve with Indian pickle.

AVOCADO & CHICKPEA WRAPS

Wraps look interesting and make a pleasant change from ordinary sandwiches. Flour tortillas make the best wrapper but large supermarkets often stock other types of flatbreads made especially for wraps as these have become popular. If wholemeal/whole-wheat tortillas are available, they are the best choice.

4 wholemeal/whole-wheat tortillas or other wraps

400-g/14-oz. can chickpeas drained and rinsed

4 generous spoonfuls cottage cheese

1 ripe avocado, thinly sliced

1 tomato, deseeded and flesh diced

3–4 tablespoons grated Cheddar

a few handfuls of shredded Little Gem/Bibb lettuce and/or sprouted seeds

a little freshly squeezed lemon juice

rapeseed/canola oil or extra virgin olive oil, for drizzling

sea salt and freshly ground black pepper, to season

SERVES 2–4

Working one at a time, put a tortilla on the work surface. Sprinkle a quarter of the chickpeas on top, in a line down the middle. Mash lightly with a fork, spreading out in a half-moon shape towards one edge of the tortilla.

Cover this with a generous spoonful of cottage cheese. Arrange a few avocado slices on top, in a line down the middle. Sprinkle over a small handful of diced tomato, a little grated Cheddar and some lettuce. Squeeze over a little lemon juice, season lightly and finish with a drizzle of oil.

Starting from the edge with the filling, begin rolling to enclose the filling. Cut the wrap in half and serve immediately, with the seam-side down.

LEEK & CHICKPEAS WITH MUSTARD DRESSING (pictured)

This is a relaxed dish to serve with meat or fish, or as an appetizer with sourdough on the side. This is best made in advance to let the flavours sit!

5 tablespoons rapeseed/canola oil
4 medium leeks, washed well and finely chopped
sea salt, to season
400 g/3 cups cooked chickpeas (see page 4), ⅓ crushed to absorb more flavour
a handful of fresh flat-leaf parsley, finely chopped
freshly ground black pepper, to season
1 tablespoon Dijon mustard
1 teaspoon wholegrain mustard
1 tablespoon white wine vinegar

SERVES 4-6

Heat 2 tablespoons of the oil in a frying pan/skillet, add the leeks and salt to taste and cook until softened. Add the chickpeas, mix well and heat well together. Take off the heat and add the parsley and black pepper.

Mix the mustards, vinegar and remaining oil together, then stir into the leeks and chickpeas and serve.

CHICKPEA, EGG & POTATO SALAD

A pleasing combination of flavours and textures, the chickpeas are bound together by the broken-up potato, hard-boiled egg and oily dressing.

250 g/1½ cups cooked chickpeas (see page 4), drained and rinsed
500 g/1 lb. 2 oz. salad potatoes, boiled and bashed gently
a handful of olives, green or black
3 hard-boiled/cooked eggs, peeled and roughly chopped
freshly chopped chives

VINAIGRETTE
4 tablespoons olive oil
1 tablespoon white wine vinegar
1 tablespoon freshly chopped parsley
1 garlic clove, crushed
salt and freshly ground black pepper, to season

SERVES 4

Make the vinaigrette by whisking all the ingredients together in a bowl with a fork or a balloon whisk.

Mash some of the chickpeas slightly, then mix them with the whole chickpeas and the potatoes. Add the olives and vinaigrette and stir well.

Distribute the chopped eggs through the salad, taking care not to break them up too much. Sprinkle chopped chives over the surface and serve.

QUINOA TABBOULEH WITH SPINACH FALAFEL

A Middle Eastern-themed dish, packed with spice.

300 g/2 cups dried
   chickpeas, soaked in cold
   water overnight
sea salt and freshly ground
   black pepper, to season

TABBOULEH
170 g/1 cup quinoa
500 ml/2 cups vegan stock
   (made from stock cubes
   or bouillon powder)
1 small red onion
100 g/3½ oz. baby plum
   tomatoes
1 red (bell) pepper
a handful of flat-leaf parsley
freshly squeezed juice of
   1 lime

HUMMUS
4 tablespoons olive oil
2 tablespoons raw tahini
1 garlic clove
freshly squeezed juice of
   1 lemon
1 teaspoon paprika
1 teaspoon chopped red
   chilli/chile
a handful of coriander/
   cilantro, freshly chopped

SPINACH FALAFEL
75 g/2½ cups spinach
7 tablespoons olive oil
125 g/1 cup chickpea/gram
   flour
½ teaspoon chopped red
   chilli/chile

SERVES 4

To make the tabbouleh, rinse the quinoa under running water, then place in a pan with the stock. Bring to the boil, simmer for 20 minutes, then turn off the heat and fork through to distribute any remaining stock. This will be absorbed as the quinoa cools.

Drain the chickpeas from their soaking water and rinse. Place in a pan and cover with water. Bring to the boil and cook for at least 30 minutes or until tender. Drain and rinse under cold water to cool.

To make the hummus, place a third of the cooled chickpeas in a blender with the olive oil, tahini, garlic, lemon juice, paprika, chilli/chile, and coriander/cilantro. Add 60 ml/¼ cup water and blend well. Season to taste. Tip into a bowl, cover and place in the fridge.

Complete the tabbouleh by chopping the onion, tomatoes, pepper and parsley. Place in a salad bowl and stir through the quinoa. Squeeze over the lime juice and season to taste. Cover and place in the fridge while you prepare the falafel.

To make the falafel, roughly chop the spinach and place in a large bowl. Add the remaining chickpeas, 5 tablespoons of olive oil, the chickpea/gram flour, chilli/chile, and 2 tablespoons of water and blend with a hand blender. Season to taste. Form into 8 small patties, about 8 cm/3¼ in. in diameter and 2 cm/¾ in. thick.

Heat the remaining 2 tablespoons olive oil in a large frying pan/ skillet. Add the falafel to the hot oil (you may need to do this in batches). Fry over a medium heat for 5–7 minutes on each side until well browned and hot all the way through.

Serve with the hummus, tabbouleh, lime wedges and extra olive oil, for drizzling.

HONEY-ROASTED CARROTS & CHICKPEAS WITH CITRUS CREAM

Sweet, sticky and spicy, here carrots are combined with chickpeas and toasted seeds, and served with a fragrant cream made with fresh orange zest and juice mixed with crème fraîche.

600 g/1 lb. 5 oz. baby carrots, scrubbed and trimmed
3 tablespoons extra virgin olive oil, plus extra for drizzling
2 tablespoons balsamic vinegar
1 teaspoon cumin seeds
2 teaspoons clear honey
400-g/14-oz. can chickpeas, drained and rinsed
2 large handfuls of rocket/arugula leaves
1 red chilli/chile, deseeded and thinly sliced
2 handfuls of basil leaves
4 tablespoons mixed sunflower and pumpkin seeds, toasted
sea salt and freshly ground black pepper, to season

CITRUS CREAM
100 ml/⅓ cup crème fraîche
finely grated zest of ½ orange
3 tablespoons freshly squeezed orange juice

SERVES 4

Preheat the oven to 200°C (400°F) Gas 6.

Put the carrots in a large roasting pan and drizzle over enough oil to coat, season, then toss them with your hands. Roast the carrots in the preheated oven for 15 minutes, then stir in the balsamic vinegar and sprinkle the cumin seeds over. Return the carrots to the oven for another 15 minutes or until tender and starting to turn golden.

Meanwhile, for the citrus cream mix together the crème fraîche, the orange zest and half the juice in a bowl. Transfer the carrots to another bowl. Stir the honey and remaining orange juice into the juices in the roasting pan until combined and then pour over the carrots. Add the chickpeas, rocket/arugula and chilli/chile and toss until mixed together. Divide between 4 serving plates and arrange the basil leaves and toasted seeds over.

Top each serving with a spoonful of the citrus cream.

CHICKPEA SALAD WITH ONIONS & PAPRIKA

Packed with nutrition, this dish is particularly good served warm.

225 g/1¼ cups dried chickpeas, soaked in cold water overnight
1 red onion, cut in half lengthways, then in half crossways and sliced with the grain
4 garlic cloves, finely chopped
1 teaspoon ground cumin
1–2 teaspoons paprika
3 tablespoons olive oil
freshly squeezed juice of 1 lemon
leaves from a small bunch each of fresh flat-leaf parsley and coriander/cilantro, coarsely chopped
125 g/4½ oz. firm goat's cheese or feta cheese, crumbled (optional)
sea salt and freshly ground black pepper, to season
crusty bread, to serve

SERVES 4

Drain the chickpeas and put them in a deep saucepan. Cover with water and bring to the boil. Reduce the heat and simmer for about 45 minutes, until the chickpeas are tender but not mushy.

Drain the warm chickpeas and tip into a bowl. Add the onion, garlic, cumin and paprika and toss in the olive oil and lemon juice while the chickpeas are still warm, making sure they are all well coated. Season with salt and pepper to taste and toss in most of the parsley and coriander/cilantro. Crumble over the goat's cheese, if using, and sprinkle with the rest of the herbs.

Serve while still warm with chunks of crusty bread.

LUSCIOUS UNDONE FALAFEL SALAD

If you've never baked chickpeas in the oven, give this a try! Quick and easy, you can enjoy the flavours of falafel, without the hassle of deep-frying.

MEDITERRANEAN SEED FALAFEL MIXTURE
120 g/1 cup pumpkin seeds
70 g/½ cup sunflower seeds
60 g/½ cup walnuts
6 sun-dried tomato halves, soaked
50 g/½ cup fresh basil leaves
50 g/½ cup fresh flat-leaf parsley leaves
½ teaspoon dried oregano
½ teaspoon mix of Mediterranean dried herbs (thyme, marjoram, rosemary, basil, fennel)
2 garlic cloves, crushed
1–2 tablespoons olive oil
1 tablespoon freshly squeezed lemon juice, or to taste
salt, to taste

TO SERVE
tzatziki
4 pitta pockets, cut into wedges, toasted, to serve

baking sheet, lined with parchment paper

SERVES 2-4

BAKED CHICKPEAS
2 tablespoons tamari
¼ teaspoon chilli/chili powder
¼ teaspoon ground turmeric
¼ teaspoon ground ginger
½ teaspoon ground coriander
¼ teaspoon ground cumin
1 tablespoon olive oil
160 g/1 cup cooked chickpeas, drained (see page 4)

SALAD
20 g/1 cup rocket/arugula
1 round/butterhead lettuce (about 160 g/5½ oz.)
6 leaves red leaf lettuce
2 ripe tomatoes (about 340 g/12 oz.)
1 small bunch of fresh basil
2 tablespoons olive oil
2 tablespoons red wine vinegar

For the Mediterranean Seed Falafel Mixture, grind the seeds and walnuts into fine flour. Chop the tomatoes very finely. Add the chopped tomatoes, together with the remaining ingredients, to the seed flour and mix well with your hands or with a silicone spatula. Wrap in clingfilm/plastic wrap and let sit in the fridge for 30 minutes.

For the Baked Chickpeas, preheat the oven to 180°C (350°F) Gas 4. Mix together all the ingredients apart from the chickpeas to make a marinade. Pour the marinade over the chickpeas and toss to coat well. Spread the coated chickpeas on the prepared baking sheet and bake in the preheated oven for 15–20 minutes until they soak in all the marinade and start browning.

Wash the salad leaves well and drain or spin. Tear the lettuce leaves into smaller pieces. Cut the tomatoes into wedges and chop the basil. Place all the vegetables in a big wide bowl, crumble over the Mediterranean Seed Falafel mixture, add the baked chickpeas and drizzle with olive oil and vinegar. Mix well to incorporate.

Divide into separate plates and serve the tzatziki, so each person can add a few blobs to the falafel salad just before eating.

CHARGRILLED HALLOUMI, COURGETTE & CHICKPEA SALAD

Pomegranate molasses, a popular ingredient in Middle Eastern cooking, lends a tangy, sweet-sour flavour to the dressing for this main meal salad. It also makes a useful base for a marinade and goes particularly well with bean and vegetable dishes.

125 g/4 oz. rocket/arugula leaves

600-g/1-lb. 5-oz. can chickpeas, drained and rinsed

1 small red onion, sliced

1 courgette/zucchini, coarsely grated

400 g/14 oz. halloumi cheese, patted dry and sliced

seeds from ½ pomegranate

4 tablespoons freshly chopped mint leaves

POMEGRANATE MOLASSES DRESSING

4 tablespoons extra virgin olive oil, plus extra for brushing

2 tablespoons pomegranate molasses

1 teaspoon freshly squeezed lemon juice

½ teaspoon caster/ granulated sugar

sea salt and freshly ground black pepper, to season

SERVES 4

Mix together all the ingredients for the dressing and season with salt and pepper.

Divide the rocket/arugula, chickpeas, red onion and courgette/zucchini between 4 serving plates. Spoon enough of the dressing over the salad to lightly coat it and toss gently until everything is combined.

Heat a large, ridged griddle pan over a high heat.

Brush the halloumi slices with a little extra olive oil. Reduce the heat a little and griddle the halloumi for 2 minutes on each side or until slightly blackened in places and softened.

Serve the halloumi on top of the salad, garnished with the pomegranate seeds and mint.

CHICKPEA, SQUASH & SPINACH SALAD WITH DUKKAH

Dukkah – a fragrant Egyptian mix of spices, nuts, seeds and dried chilli/hot red pepper flakes – is delicious sprinkled over salads or roasted vegetables.

1 teaspoon smoked hot paprika
1 tablespoon extra-virgin olive oil
400 g/14 oz. butternut squash, peeled, seeded and sliced into wedges
150 g/5 oz. baby spinach leaves, tough stalks trimmed
2 avocados, peeled, halved, stoned/pitted and cubed
400-g/14-oz. can chickpeas, drained and rinsed
1 small red onion, diced
a large handful of coriander/cilantro leaves
2 tablespoons dukkah (see below)

LEMON & CORIANDER DRESSING
1 teaspoon coriander seeds
5 tablespoons extra virgin olive oil
finely grated zest and freshly squeezed juice of 1 small lemon
sea salt and freshly ground black pepper, to season

SERVES 4

DUKKAH
3 tablespoons coriander seeds
2 teaspoons cumin seeds
2 tablespoons sesame seeds
3 tablespoons sunflower seeds
3 tablespoons pumpkin seeds
40 g/⅓ cup hazelnuts
40 g/⅓ cup blanched almonds
½ teaspoon dried chilli/hot red pepper flakes
sea salt and freshly ground black pepper, to season

For the dukkah, put all the seeds in a dry frying pan/skillet and toast for 2–3 minutes, shaking the pan occasionally, until they are aromatic and start colouring. Tip out of the pan and let cool. Next, add the nuts to the pan and cook for 5 minutes, shaking the pan occasionally, until they smell toasted and start to colour. Tip out of the pan and let cool. Put the toasted seeds and nuts in a mini grinder and grind to a coarse, crumbly mixture. Transfer to a bowl, stir in the dried chilli/hot red pepper flakes and season well.

Preheat the oven to 200°C (400°F) Gas 6.

Mix the paprika with the oil in a large bowl, season, stir in the squash and turn until evenly coated, then tip onto a baking sheet. Roast the squash in the preheated oven for 30–35 minutes, turning once, until tender and golden.

Meanwhile, to make the dressing, put the coriander seeds in a large, dry frying pan/skillet and toast for 2–3 minutes, shaking the pan occasionally, until they smell aromatic and start to colour. Grind using a pestle and mortar to a coarse powder. Transfer the ground coriander seeds to a bowl and mix in the oil and lemon zest and juice. Season and set aside.

Put the spinach in a large serving bowl and add the roasted squash, avocados, chickpeas, red onion and half the fresh coriander/cilantro. Pour enough of the dressing over to coat and turn gently until combined.

Just before serving, sprinkle the dukkah and the remaining fresh coriander/cilantro over the salad.

CHICKPEA & SPICED CAULIFLOWER SALAD WITH TAMARIND DRESSING

Cauliflower takes on a new lease of life when marinated in spices and roasted until just tender. Here, it is served on top of an Indian-inspired chickpea, tomato and potato salad with a tangy dressing.

3 tablespoons cold pressed rapeseed/canola oil or light olive oil

2 teaspoons ground turmeric

2 tablespoons tikka curry paste

freshly squeezed juice of ½ lime

1 cauliflower, cut into florets, stalks trimmed

400-g/14-oz. new potatoes, halved

400-g/14-oz. can chickpeas, drained and rinsed

1 small red onion, diced

4 tomatoes, deseeded and diced

2 large handfuls of coriander/cilantro leaves, freshly chopped

sea salt and freshly ground black pepper, to season

TAMARIND DRESSING

3 tablespoons tamarind paste

2.5-cm/1-in. piece of fresh ginger, peeled and diced

freshly squeezed juice of ½ lime

6 tablespoons natural/plain yogurt

SERVES 4

Preheat the oven to 200°C (400°F) Gas 6.

Mix together the oil, turmeric, curry paste and lime juice in a shallow bowl, then season. Add the cauliflower and turn to coat in the paste. Transfer to a roasting pan and roast in the preheated oven for 10–15 minutes, depending on the size of the florets, turning once, until tender.

Meanwhile, cook the potatoes in a pan of boiling water for 12–15 minutes, until tender. Drain and leave until cool enough to handle, then peel off the skins and cut into cubes.

Mix together all the ingredients for the dressing, and season with salt and pepper.

Put the potatoes in a serving bowl with the chickpeas, onion, tomatoes and half the coriander/cilantro. Spoon the dressing over and mix gently until combined. Top with the roasted cauliflower and the remaining coriander/cilantro.

3

CURRIES, SHEET PANS & CASSEROLES

CHICKPEA 'TIKKA' MASALA

The Indian takeout staple gets a vegan makeover with chickpeas in a lush tomato-based sauce. Serve with fluffy rice, chopped chilli/chile, fresh herbs and naan breads on the side for a simple and satisfying feast.

coconut oil, for frying
1 onion, finely diced
1 yellow (bell) pepper,
    deseeded and finely
    chopped
2 garlic cloves, finely
    chopped
2 teaspoons garam masala
1 teaspoon ground cumin
½ teaspoon ground
    turmeric
2 carrots, peeled and finely
    chopped
2 x 400-g/14-oz. cans
    chickpeas, drained and
    rinsed
2 x 400-g/14-oz. cans finely
    chopped tomatoes in
    juice or crushed tomatoes
400-g/14-oz. can coconut
    milk
¼ teaspoon cayenne pepper
    (optional)
salt, to taste

TO SERVE (OPTIONAL)
cooked brown rice or
    quinoa
naan breads
freshly chopped coriander/
    cilantro leaves
freshly chopped chilli/chile

SERVES 6

Heat enough coconut oil to generously coat the bottom of a large saucepan over a medium-high heat. Add the onion and (bell) pepper and season with salt. Cook, stirring, for about 10 minutes.

Add the garlic and cook for 1 minute. Add the garam masala, cumin and turmeric and cook for another 30 seconds, until fragrant. Add the carrots, chickpeas and tomatoes. Bring to the boil, then reduce to a simmer and cover with a lid. Simmer for about 15–20 minutes.

Stir in the coconut milk, then simmer for 5 minutes more and remove from the heat. Stir in the cayenne pepper, if using. Let the curry stand, covered with a lid to keep warm, for at least 15 minutes to let the flavours mingle.

Serve over brown rice or quinoa, with naan breads, fresh herbs and chilli/chile, as desired.

FALAFEL COCONUT CURRY

This is a great way to use up those leftover falafels sitting in the fridge! Since traditional falafels usually contain coriander/cilantro, they go well with Indian curry spices. Chickpea patties also add satisfying texture, and transform a light vegetable curry into a heartier and more filling meal.

2 tablespoons virgin coconut oil
1 large onion, finely chopped
1 carrot, chopped into bite-size pieces
1 celery stick/rib, chopped
2-cm/¾-in. piece of fresh ginger, peeled and finely chopped
2 garlic cloves, chopped
1½ tablespoons mild curry powder
2 teaspoons ground ginger
2 teaspoons ground turmeric
2 teaspoons garam masala
¼ teaspoon chilli/chile powder, or to taste
2 tablespoons tamari soy sauce
500 ml/2 cups coconut milk (home-made or from carton, not full-fat canned milk)
½ teaspoon salt
12 leftover falafel (choose from any of the recipes in this book)
1 tablespoon kuzu, arrowroot or cornflour/cornstarch, diluted in a little cold water
chopped spring onions/scallions or coriander/cilantro, to garnish
basmati rice, chapattis or toasted pitta pockets, to serve

SERVES 4

Heat the coconut oil in a pan and sauté the onion, carrot and celery with a pinch of salt, until fragrant. Add the ginger, garlic and dry spices, combine and fry for another minute. Add the soy sauce and stir. Add enough coconut milk to cover the vegetables and bring to the boil, then add the salt, lower the heat and simmer until the vegetables are soft. Add more coconut milk if necessary.

At the end of cooking, add the leftover falafel and diluted thickener of choice (if needed), and let the curry come to the boil one last time. Adjust the seasoning to taste. Garnish with chopped spring onions/scallions or coriander/cilantro and serve with basmati rice, chapatis or toasted pitta pockets.

CHICKPEA, KALE & COCONUT KORMA

This korma is a prime example of modern Indian cuisine. It is nothing like what you would find in any Indian home or restaurant. It is the product of an Indian heritage and an appreciation of current food trends.

5 tablespoons vegetable oil
2 cloves
3 cardamom pods
½ teaspoon cumin seeds
2 large onions, finely diced
1 teaspoon salt
1 teaspoon Holy Trinity Paste (see below)
1 teaspoon ground cumin
1 teaspoon ground coriander
1 teaspoon ground turmeric
1 teaspoon tomato purée/paste
3 tablespoons ground almonds
2 tablespoons unsweetened desiccated/shredded dried coconut
1 teaspoon caster/granulated sugar
200 ml/¾ cup coconut milk
240 g/1¾ cups canned chickpeas, drained and rinsed
100 g/3 oz. kale, chopped and tough stalks removed
1 teaspoon garam masala
naan bread or cooked rice, to serve

SERVES 4

HOLY TRINITY PASTE
200 g/7 oz. (about 6) green chillies/chiles
200 g/7 oz. (about 40) garlic cloves
200 g/7 oz. (about 8 x 5-cm/2-in. pieces) fresh ginger
50 ml/3½ tablespoons vegetable oil
1 tablespoon salt

MAKES 625 G/2½ CUPS

For the Holy Trinity Paste, blitz together the ingredients in a food processor to form a coarse paste. Store in the fridge for up to 2 weeks.

Heat the vegetable oil in a heavy-based pan over a medium heat, add the cloves and cardamom pods and allow to heat until you can see the spices sizzling. Add the cumin seeds and allow them to sizzle and crackle in the pan. Add the onions and salt and fry until softened. This will take 25–30 minutes; it is best to cover the onions with a lid to prevent browning.

When the onions are completely softened and buttery, add the Holy Trinity Paste and cook through until it no longer smells raw. Add the ground spices and mix well. If the pan is starting to dry out, add a splash of water to loosen the mix. Cook the spices for 3–5 minutes.

Next, add the tomato purée/paste and mix well. Again, if the pan is drying out, add another splash of water. Once the tomato purée is completely mixed in with the other ingredients, add the ground almonds, dried coconut and sugar and mix well. Pour in 200 ml/¾ cup of water to make the 'base' of your korma sauce. Add the coconut milk, mix well and leave to simmer for 3–4 minutes.

Add the chickpeas, mix well and leave to simmer for 3 minutes. Add the kale and stir into the sauce for 1 minute. Sprinkle over the garam masala, stir in and remove from the heat.

Serve with naan bread or rice.

CHANA SAAG PANEER

Canned spinach makes quick work of this popular Indian curry, comprising chickpeas, spinach and paneer. It's great to keep canned chickpeas and spinach in the kitchen cupboard for this recipe. This is delicious on its own, but feel free to serve with warmed naan breads or plain basmati rice and topped with a dollop of mango chutney.

380-g/13½-oz. can leaf spinach
250-g/9-oz. pack paneer cheese (or halloumi will work too)
1 tablespoon ground cumin
a splash of olive oil
1 teaspoon cumin seeds
1 teaspoon fennel seeds
2 onions, diced
½ teaspoon ground turmeric
1 tablespoon garam masala
2.5-cm/1-in. piece of fresh ginger, peeled and grated
4 garlic cloves, chopped
2 dried whole red chillies/chiles (or a pinch of chilli/hot red pepper flakes)
400-g/14-oz. can chickpeas, drained and rinsed
1 tablespoon tomato purée/paste
1 teaspoon salt
½ x 400-g/14-oz. can coconut milk

TO SERVE
lime wedges, for squeezing
boiled rice or naan bread
mango chutney (optional)

SERVES 2 AS A MAIN OR 4 AS A SIDE

Start with the spinach: pour the contents of the can into a sieve/strainer and use the back of a spoon to push down on the spinach, extracting as much liquid as possible. Leave this sitting in the sieve/strainer over a bowl while you prepare the rest of the ingredients.

Cut the paneer cheese into 2.5-cm/1-in. cubes and dust with half the ground cumin. Heat a splash of oil in a frying pan/skillet over a high heat, add the paneer and fry for just a couple of minutes until golden, then remove from the pan.

Add a splash more oil to the pan along with the cumin and fennel seeds and sweat the diced onions for about 6 minutes until caramelised and golden. Add the remaining spices, ginger, garlic and chillies/chiles and cook for 30 seconds, then add the drained chickpeas and tomato purée/paste. Tip in the spinach with the salt and stir to incorporate it with the rest of the ingredients. Fold in half a can of coconut milk, warm through until it bubbles, stirring frequently, then remove from the heat.

Serve in bowls with a wedge of lime and some boiled rice or a chunk of ripped naan for company; a swirl of the remaining coconut milk over the top is a nice touch.

CHICKPEA SATAY CURRY

This is very simple to make, is packed with plant protein and is creamy and delicious with the peanut butter and coconut milk.

2 teaspoons sesame or peanut oil
2 garlic cloves, crushed
1 onion, diced
150 g/2 cups prepped vegetables (such as peas, beans and/or broccoli)
400-g/14-oz. can chickpeas, drained and rinsed
160 ml/⅔ cup coconut milk

1–2 tablespoons tamari sauce
125 g/½ cup peanut butter
freshly squeezed juice of 1 lime
basmati or brown rice, to serve
coriander/cilantro leaves, chopped peanuts and sliced chilli/chile, to serve (optional)

SERVES 4

In a pan, heat the oil and cook the garlic and onion for a few minutes. Add in the vegetables, stir to combine and cook on a low heat with the lid on until partly cooked. Add the chickpeas and stir.

For the sauce, combine the coconut milk, tamari and peanut butter in a bowl and whisk with a fork. Pour into the curry and mix. Cook on a low heat for 5 minutes. Squeeze over the lime juice and top with the remaining ingredients. Serve with cooked rice.

CHICKPEA & SPINACH TAGINE WITH YOGURT (pictured)

This village tagine is usually served with freshly griddled flatbreads, or a warm crusty loaf.

1 tablespoon ghee, smen or argan oil, or 1 tablespoon olive oil plus 1 tablespoon butter
1 onion, finely chopped
2 garlic cloves, finely chopped
a thumb-sized piece of fresh ginger, peeled and finely chopped
1 teaspoon cumin seeds
250 g/1½ cups cooked chickpeas (see page 4)
1 teaspoon ground turmeric

1–2 teaspoons ras el hanout (see page 116)
500 g/1 lb. 2 oz. spinach, steamed and roughly chopped
2–3 tablespoons thick, creamy yogurt
½ teaspoon paprika
sea salt and freshly ground black pepper, to season

SERVES 3-4

Heat the ghee in the base of a tagine or a heavy-based saucepan, add the onion, garlic, ginger and cumin seeds and sauté until they begin to colour. Toss in the chickpeas, coating them in the onion mixture, and stir in the ground turmeric and ras el hanout. Add the spinach and 150 ml/⅔ cup water. Put the lid on the tagine and cook over a gentle heat for 10–15 minutes.

Season the tagine with salt and pepper, swirl in the yogurt, dust with the paprika and serve immediately.

SPICED CHICKPEA, TOMATO & ALMOND CURRY

This recipe makes a fabulously tasty, reasonably inexpensive but very healthy weekday supper. It is super quick to make too, especially if you use canned chickpeas, and can be rustled up from things you most likely already have in your fridge and storecupboard. The ground almonds give the sauce a rich creamy texture, as well as adding extra protein. Serve with warmed chapatis or naan breads and mango chutney, plus a dollop of cooling yogurt or a non-dairy alternative, if you fancy it.

2 onions, sliced
4–5 tablespoons olive oil
2 teaspoons garam masala
1 teaspoon ground turmeric
1 teaspoon ground coriander
1 teaspoon ground cumin
1 teaspoon dried chilli/hot red pepper flakes
60 g/2¼ oz. fresh ginger
2 garlic cloves, finely chopped
2 x 400-g/14-oz. cans chopped tomatoes
2 x 400-g/14-oz. cans chickpeas, drained and rinsed
2 tablespoons good-quality tomato ketchup
80 g/¾ cup ground almonds
freshly chopped coriander/ cilantro leaves
1 red chilli/chile, deseeded and sliced, to garnish

SERVES 4

Preheat the oven to 190°C (375°F) Gas 5.

Scatter the onion slices over the base of a deep sheet pan and drizzle with the olive oil. Add the garam masala, turmeric, ground coriander, cumin and chilli/hot red pepper flakes. Stir to coat the onions in the spices. Roast for 10 minutes.

Peel the ginger and cut it into julienne. Remove the pan from the oven and add the ginger and chopped garlic. Stir in the chopped tomatoes, chickpeas, tomato ketchup and ground almonds. Return the pan to the oven and cook for about 20–25 minutes, until the sauce is lovely and thickened.

Serve garnished with chopped coriander/cilantro and red chilli/ chile slices.

CHICKPEA & MUSHROOM FREEKEH PILAF

With its subtle smoky flavour, freekeh (made from young durum wheat) is a great grain to cook with. Here, it is combined with nutty chickpeas and earthy mushrooms to make an appealing, colourful Middle Eastern pilaf.

1 tablespoon butter
1 red onion, ½ chopped,
   ½ sliced
½ cinnamon stick
3 cardamom pods
½ tablespoon coriander
   seeds
250 g/1¼ cups freekeh
   (roasted green durum
   wheat), rinsed
400 ml/1⅔ cups vegetable
   stock
1 tablespoon olive oil
1 garlic clove, chopped
250 g/8 oz. white/cup
   mushrooms, sliced
   1-cm/⅜-in. thick
400-g/14-oz. can chickpeas,
   drained and rinsed
salt, to season
4 tablespoons pomegranate
   seeds, to garnish
freshly chopped coriander/
   cilantro, to garnish

SERVES 4

Heat the butter in a heavy-based saucepan. Add the chopped red onion, cinnamon stick, cardamom and coriander seeds and fry, stirring a little, over a gentle heat for 2–3 minutes.

Add the freekeh, mixing well to coat in the flavoured butter. Add the stock and season with salt. Bring to the boil. Cover, reduce the heat and simmer for 20–25 minutes over a very low heat until the stock has reduced and the freekeh grains have softened.

Heat the olive oil in a frying pan/skillet. Fry the sliced red onion and garlic over a medium heat for 2 minutes, until softened and fragrant. Add the mushrooms and fry over a high heat, stirring, until lightly browned.

Fold two-thirds of the chickpeas into the freekeh. Place the mixture in a serving dish. Top with the freshly fried mushrooms and remaining chickpeas. Sprinkle with the pomegranate seeds and coriander/cilantro to garnish. Serve at once.

VEGAN BAKED CHICKPEA FAJITAS

Fajitas seem like the best party food to serve to a crowd. Making up your own fajita whilst sat around a table with your friends or family is such a sociable way to enjoy a meal!

2 medium sweet potatoes, peeled and chopped into 1.5-cm/½-in. pieces
3 teaspoons olive oil
2 (bell) peppers, ideally different colours, deseeded and cut into 2-cm/¾-in. long slices
2 red onions, sliced into thin wedges
28-g/1-oz. packet of fajita seasoning mix
400-g/14-oz. can chickpeas, drained and rinsed
avocado mayonnaise (see below) or coconut yogurt, to serve
wraps or steamed rice, to serve

AVOCADO MAYONNAISE
3 ripe avocados, pitted/ stoned and skin removed
1 tablespoon freshly squeezed lemon juice
1 tablespoon apple cider vinegar
2 tablespoons olive oil
sea salt and freshly ground black pepper, to season

SERVES 4

Preheat the oven to 200°C (400°F) Gas 6.

Put the sweet potatoes on a large sheet pan with sides. Drizzle over ½ teaspoon of the olive oil. Bake in the preheated oven for 15 minutes.

Meanwhile, mix the peppers, onions, remaining 2½ teaspoons olive oil and the fajita seasoning together in a bowl.

Once the sweet potatoes have been baking for 15 minutes, add the pepper and onion mix to the sheet pan and stir. Bake for another 15 minutes, then add the chickpeas for the last minute and stir well.

To make the avocado mayonnaise, put all the ingredients except the olive oil into a food processor and process to a paste. Add the olive oil and process again. Adjust the lemon juice, vinegar and salt and pepper to your preferred taste.

Serve the fajitas with avocado mayonnaise or coconut yogurt and either wraps or rice.

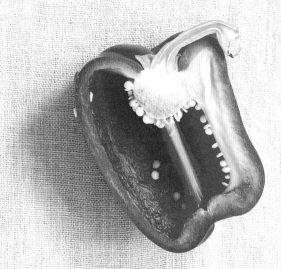

HEAT & EAT FALAFEL CASSEROLE

Vegan cheese works well in this recipe – it's hard to resist the melted cheese in comforting casserole-style dishes! This is something different which everybody will enjoy.

230 ml/1 cup tomato sauce
 (see below)
7–9 leftover falafel (choose any
 from the recipes in this book)
50 g/½ cup grated white Cheddar-
 style vegan or vegetarian cheese
 that melts well
olive oil, to drizzle
blanched broccoli or any other
 greens, to serve
toasted sourdough bread or
 creamy mashed potatoes,
 to serve

TOMATO SAUCE
3 tablespoons extra virgin olive oil
1 large onion, finely chopped
1 teaspoon vegetable bouillon
 powder or ½ bouillon cube
 (optional)
1 teaspoon dried oregano or basil
1 tablespoon rice, agave or maple
 syrup
1 tablespoon tamari soy sauce
230 ml/1 cup tomato passata/
 strained tomatoes
2 garlic cloves, crushed
2 tablespoons freshly chopped
 parsley or snipped chives
salt and freshly ground black
 pepper, to taste

MAKES ABOUT 375 ML/1½ CUPS

large baking dish

SERVES 2-3

Start by making the tomato sauce. Heat the olive oil in a pan over a medium heat and sauté the onion until translucent. Add the bouillon powder/cube, herbs, syrup and tamari, and stir until the onion soaks up the spices; about 2 minutes.

Add the passata/strained tomatoes and bring it to the boil. Now lower the heat and leave to simmer, uncovered, for about 10 minutes, or until thick. At the very end of cooking, add the garlic, parsley or chives and an extra drop of olive oil. Season to taste. This sauce can be made a couple of days in advance and kept refrigerated, if needed.

To assemble the casserole, preheat the oven to 180°C (350°F) Gas 4.

Drizzle a little bit of olive oil in the bottom of the baking dish, pour in the tomato sauce, add a layer of leftover falafel and cover with grated cheese. Bake in the preheated oven for 10–15 minutes, until the tomato sauce starts sizzling and the cheese melts.

Serve with blanched broccoli or any other greens, toasted sourdough bread or creamy mashed potatoes.

CHICKPEA 'CHUNA' QUESADILLAS WITH JICAMA SLAW

This is a very quick and easy dish to prepare, and super healthy too.

CHICKPEA 'CHUNA'
400-g/14-oz. can chickpeas, drained and rinsed
4 tablespoons finely diced celery, including chopped leaves
½ red onion, finely diced
3 tablespoons hummus
freshly squeezed juice of ½ lemon
½ teaspoon garlic powder
¼ teaspoon chilli/chili powder
½ teaspoon sea salt
½ teaspoon ground white pepper
⅛ sheet of nori seaweed, blitzed or chopped to a fine crumb

JICAMA SLAW
200 g/7 oz. jicama, peeled
¼ cucumber, halved lengthways and deseeded
1 carrot, peeled
2 tablespoons rice vinegar
1 tablespoon freshly squeezed lime juice
a large pinch of sea salt

SERVES 2-4

ANCHO CHILLI & MANGO DRESSING
2 large dried ancho chillies/chiles, soaked in boiling water for 15 minutes, then drained
1 small ghost chilli/chile (or use 3–4 very hot bird's eye chillies/chiles), soaked in boiling water for 15 minutes, then drained
355 ml/1½ cups mango purée
1 teaspoon sea salt
1–2 tablespoons unrefined sugar or agave syrup

MAKES APPROX. 450 ML/2 CUPS

TO SERVE
4 large flour tortillas
Ancho Chilli/Chile & Mango Dressing (see above), or use any other chilli/chili sauce (optional)

For the dressing, add the chillies, 120 ml/½ cup water, the mango purée, salt and sugar or agave syrup to a pan. Bring to a simmer for 10 minutes, remove from the heat and purée using a stick blender. Taste the sauce and add more sugar and salt as needed. If too thick, add a little more water. Set aside at room temperature.

For the jicama slaw, slice the vegetables into 2.5-cm/1-in. thin matchsticks. Mix them together with the remaining ingredients in a small bowl. Set aside for 10 minutes.

For the chickpea 'chuna', mash the chickpeas with a fork in a small bowl. Add all the remaining ingredients and mix well. Set aside.

For the quesadillas, put a large frying pan/skillet over a medium-high heat, and put a large tortilla in the pan. Add 2–3 generous tablespoons of the chickpea mixture into the centre and fold the tortilla in half, pressing down slightly to spread the mixture out inside but without spilling out of the edges. Toast for a minute or two, then carefully turn over and toast on the second side for another minute. Slide the quesadilla onto a chopping board and slice to serve. Repeat with the remaining tortillas and chickpea mixture.

Serve with a heap of jicama slaw on top, and drizzle with the chilli dressing or sauce, if you like.

SPICY CARROT & CHICKPEA TAGINE WITH TURMERIC & CORIANDER

Chickpeas and other pulses often feature in the tagines of arid areas and poorer communities as they provide protein and nourishment where meat is scarce. Combined with vegetables and spices, hearty tagines like this Moroccan one are also popular in the street stalls and cafés of Marrakesh.

2 tablespoons ghee or smen, or 1 tablespoon olive oil plus 1 tablespoon butter

1 large onion, finely chopped

1–2 red chillies/chiles deseeded and finely chopped

2–3 garlic cloves, finely chopped

2 teaspoons cumin seeds

2 teaspoons coriander seeds

1–2 teaspoons sugar

2–3 carrots, peeled, halved lengthways and thickly sliced

2 x 400-g/14-oz. cans chickpeas, drained and rinsed

2 teaspoons ground turmeric

1 teaspoon ground cinnamon

a bunch of fresh coriander/cilantro leaves, finely chopped

sea salt and freshly ground black pepper, to season

SERVES 4

Heat the ghee in the base of a tagine or in a heavy-based saucepan, stir in the onion, chillies/chiles, garlic, cumin and coriander seeds and the sugar and sauté for 2–3 minutes, until the onion begins to colour. Toss in the carrot and cook for a further 1–2 minutes, then add the chickpeas.

Stir in the turmeric and cinnamon and pour in enough water to cover the base of the tagine. Bring the water to the boil, put on the lid and cook over a gentle heat for 20–25 minutes, topping up the water if necessary, until the carrots are tender.

Season the tagine with salt and pepper, stir in most of the coriander/cilantro and garnish with the remainder.

SYRIAN AUBERGINE & CHICKPEA RAGOUT

A winning combination of roasted chunks of aubergine/eggplant and nutty chickpeas, bound together in a sweet tomato and onion sauce enriched with herbs and spices, this Mediterranean dish known as *munazalit bathinjan* is at its best when served warm or at room temperature.

2 medium aubergines/eggplants weighing about 500 g/ 1 lb. 2 oz. in total
4 tablespoons olive oil
1 large onion, finely sliced
4 garlic cloves, finely sliced
½ teaspoon ground cinnamon
¼ teaspoon freshly grated nutmeg
a generous bunch of flat-leaf parsley, chopped
4 tomatoes, peeled and chopped
250 g/1½ cups cooked chickpeas (see page 4), or a 400-g/14-oz. can, drained and rinsed
2 tablespoons freshly chopped mint
a generous bunch of fresh coriander/cilantro, chopped
salt and freshly ground black pepper, to season
yogurt and crusty bread, to serve

SERVES 6

Preheat the oven to 180°C/350°F/Gas 4.

Cut the aubergines/eggplants into 2-cm/¾-inch cubes, and toss in half of the olive oil, then spread out on a baking sheet and roast in the preheated oven for about 20 minutes, turning the pieces over once halfway through cooking, until fairly soft.

Meanwhile, over a gentle heat, soften the sliced onion and garlic in the remaining olive oil, adding a couple of tablespoons of water if necessary to prevent browning. This should take about 20 minutes, until the onions are golden and melting.

Add the spices, stir around for a minute or two to blend the flavours, then tip in the parsley, chopped tomato and cooked aubergine/eggplant, followed by the drained chickpeas. Add about 200 ml/¾ cup water, bring to the boil and simmer, covered, for 20–30 minutes.

Take off the heat, stir in the fresh mint, adjust the seasoning and set aside for an hour or two before serving. In fact, the dish keeps perfectly well for a good 24 hours, and may even improve, and can be easily reheated.

Season with salt and pepper, sprinkle with chopped coriander/cilantro, and serve warm. A spoonful of yogurt and crusty bread make good accompaniments.

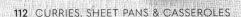

CHICKPEA RATATOUILLE STEW

This is a quick version of ratatouille, with added chickpeas for an extra serving of legumes to make it a healthy, nutritious plant-based dinner. Serve with cooked quinoa, couscous or brown rice.

3 garlic cloves, crushed
1 onion, diced
1 tablespoon olive oil
1 teaspoon dried Italian
 herbs
quinoa or brown rice,
 to serve
1 large courgette/zucchini,
 sliced
1 red (bell) pepper,
 deseeded and diced
1 aubergine/eggplant, diced
400-g/14-oz. can chopped
 tomatoes or same weight
 of fresh diced tomatoes
 or passata/strained
 tomatoes
400-g/14-oz. can chickpeas,
 drained and rinsed
salt and freshly ground
 black pepper, to season
baby spinach and basil
 leaves, to serve (optional)

SERVES 4

In a large pot over a medium heat, cook the garlic and onion in the olive oil along with the dried herbs. Cook for 5 minutes, stirring often, until the onion is soft and translucent.

Meanwhile, cook the quinoa or rice following the packet instructions.

Add the vegetables and tomatoes to the onion and garlic. Stir to combine and then cook, covered with a lid and stirring often, for 10–20 minutes until the vegetables are soft. Add the chickpeas and stir to combine.

Season with salt and pepper. Serve alongside the quinoa or rice, with baby spinach and basil (if using).

MOROCCAN CHICKPEA PUMPKIN STEW

This North African-influenced dish is a great way to introduce a sweetness that negates the craving for dessert. You can easily purchase ras el hanout spice blend or make your own, as below.

2 tablespoons coconut or rapeseed/canola oil
1 red onion, chopped
2 garlic cloves, chopped
4 teaspoons ras el hanout (see Note)
225 g/1 cup amaranth
200 g/1½ cups dried chickpeas, cooked according to instructions on page 4
1 large sweet potato, cubed
1 pumpkin – you will need 735 g /1 lb. 10 oz. cubed flesh
¼ teaspoon sea salt
65 g/½ cup raisins
90 g/1 cup toasted slivered/flaked almonds
sea salt and freshly ground black pepper, to season
sprigs of cilantro/coriander, to garnish (optional)

SERVES 4

Gently heat the oil in a large pan, add the onion, garlic and spice and sweat over a low heat for 5 minutes.

Meanwhile, put the amaranth into a pan with 500 ml/2 cups water. Bring to the boil, then simmer for 20 minutes. Take off the heat and allow any remaining water to be absorbed.

Drain the chickpeas and add with the chopped sweet potato and pumpkin to the pan containing the onions. Cover in water, add the lid to the pan and simmer for 15 minutes. Stir thoroughly, then add the salt and raisins and simmer for a further 5 minutes. Drain the chickpeas and add to the pan.

Season the amaranth to taste and stir in three-quarters of the almonds. Serve with the pumpkin stew, garnished with the remaining almonds and sprigs of coriander/cilantro.

Note: To make your own ras el hanout spice mix, in a dry pan toast 3 tablespoons cumin seeds, 2½ tablespoons coriander seeds, 1½ tablespoons ground cinnamon, 2½ teaspoons ground ginger, 2 teaspoons black peppercorns, 1½ teaspoons ground turmeric, 1 teaspoon paprika, ½ teaspoon cardamom seeds, ½ teaspoon ground nutmeg, ¼ teaspoon cloves, and a pinch of saffron threads for a few minutes until fragrant. Grind in a spice grinder or clean coffee grinder with a few dried rose petals. Store any leftover spice mixture in an airtight jar.

CHICKPEA, CHARD & POTATO STEW

This is a homely, nourishing one-pot meal. The potatoes soak up the stock, becoming tasty and tender, contrasting well with the nutty chickpeas and the chard. Dried chickpeas have a better texture, but if time is short you can substitute a can of chickpeas in water, rinsing them and adding them in after the potatoes have simmered for 10 minutes.

120 g/¾ cup dried
   chickpeas, soaked
   overnight in water
2 tablespoons olive oil
1 onion, chopped
1 celery stick/rib, thinly
   sliced
1 red (bell) pepper,
   deseeded and chopped
   into short strips
1 teaspoon sweet smoked
   pimentón or paprika
a splash of dry white wine
300 g/10½ oz. waxy
   potatoes, quartered
400 ml/1¾ cups vegetable
   stock
200 g/7 oz. chard or
   spinach, shredded
1 tablespoon chopped
   preserved lemon
   (optional)
salt and freshly ground
   black pepper, to season

SERVES 4

Drain the soaked chickpeas. Bring a large pan of water to the boil, add in the chickpeas and cook for around 1 hour, until they are tender but retain some texture; drain.

Heat the olive oil in a frying pan/skillet. Add in the onion and fry gently over a low heat for 5 minutes, stirring often. Add in the celery and red (bell) pepper and fry for a further 3 minutes. Sprinkle over the pimentón and add in the white wine. Cook briefly, stirring, then add in the potatoes and stock. Season with salt and freshly ground black pepper. Bring to the boil, cover, reduce the heat and simmer for 20 minutes or until the potatoes are tender.

Add in the chard or spinach and the cooked chickpeas, mixing well. Cover and cook for 5 minutes, until the chard has wilted and softened. Mix in the preserved lemon (if using) and serve at once.

CHICKPEA & VEGETABLE STEW

This is a very versatile dish so you can use whatever vegetables you have to hand. Serve with plenty of couscous.

2 tablespoons olive oil
2 red onions, quartered
1 teaspoon each ground turmeric and cinnamon
½ teaspoon paprika
1-cm/¾-in. piece of fresh ginger, peeled and finely chopped
1 red chilli/chile, finely chopped
2 garlic cloves, crushed
grated zest of 1 orange
1 red and 1 yellow (bell) pepper, roughly chopped
1 sweet potato, cubed
1 aubergine/eggplant, cut into chunks
2 carrots, sliced
50 g/⅓ cup dried apricots, quartered
400-g/14-oz. can chopped tomatoes
1 tablespoon clear honey or maple syrup
400-g/14-oz. can chickpeas, drained and rinsed
500 ml/2 cups vegetable stock
a large handful of baby spinach

TO SERVE
a handful of chopped coriander/cilantro, stirred into Greek yogurt (optional)
prepared couscous

SERVES 4-6

Preheat the oven to 180°C (350°F) Gas 4.

Heat the oil in a flameproof casserole dish set over a low–medium heat. Add the onions and cook for 5 minutes. Add the turmeric, cinnamon, paprika, ginger, chilli/chile, garlic and orange zest and cook for 1 minute. Then add the peppers, sweet potato, aubergine/eggplant and carrots. Stir so that they are well covered with the spice mixture and cook for 2 minutes. Stir in the apricots, tomatoes, honey and chickpeas. Then add the vegetable stock. Bring to the boil and cook on the hob/stovetop for 2 minutes. Cover with a lid and transfer to the preheated oven to bake for 30–40 minutes.

When the stew is cooked, remove from the oven and stir in the spinach.

Spoon the tagine onto serving plates of couscous and top with chopped fresh coriander/cilantro with yogurt, if using.

CHICKPEA & PEPPER CURRY BAKE

Chickpeas and (bell) peppers combine beautifully in this dish to bring sweetness, tanginess and yet the mellowness of a substantial vegan baked meal-in-one.

5 shallots, very finely chopped
2 small garlic cloves, very finely chopped
2-cm/¾-in. piece of fresh ginger, peeled and grated
2 teaspoons ground cumin
¾ teaspoon ground coriander
1 teaspoon ground turmeric
400-g/14-oz. can tomatoes
400-g/14-oz. can coconut milk
2 teaspoons sea salt
½ yellow (bell) pepper, deseeded and thinly sliced
½ red (bell) pepper, deseeded and thinly sliced
½ orange (bell) pepper, deseeded and thinly sliced
2 x 400-g/14-oz. cans chickpeas, drained and rinsed
freshly chopped coriander/ cilantro, to serve
boiled rice, to serve

SERVES 4

Preheat the oven to 220°C (425°F) Gas 7.

Mix the shallots, garlic, ginger, spices, tomatoes, sea salt and coconut milk together in a bowl or food processor.

Put the sliced (bell) peppers on a sheet pan with sides. Pour over the coconut milk and spice mixture. Cover with foil and bake in the preheated oven for 30 minutes.

Add the chickpeas to the curry mix and stir. Return to the oven and bake for a further 5 minutes. Sprinkle over the coriander/ cilantro and serve with rice.

SWEET BAKING & DESSERTS

CHICKPEA FUDGE COOKIES

This is a great bean-based dessert that even children will enjoy, without knowing they're having chickpeas. Fudge cookies will satisfy your chocolate craving the minute you bite into one!

60 g/½ cup 70% dark/
bittersweet vegan
chocolate, chopped
160 g/1¼ cups cooked
chickpeas (see page 4)
65 g/⅓ cup sunflower or
coconut oil
200 g/¾ cup rice, maple
or agave syrup
½ teaspoon apple cider
vinegar
130 g/1 cup plain/all-purpose
flour
2 tablespoons cacao powder
½ teaspoon baking powder
½ teaspoon bicarbonate of
soda/baking soda
¼ teaspoon salt
soy milk, as needed

*baking sheet lined with
parchment paper*

MAKES 24 COOKIES

In a double-boiler, melt the chocolate and keep it over the hot water so it stays runny.

Blend the chickpeas, oil, syrup and vinegar in a food processor or blender. Add the melted chocolate and transfer to a bowl.

Preheat the oven to 180°C (360°F) Gas 4.

Take a big sieve/strainer and place it on top of the bowl with the liquid ingredients (this way you won't have to use two separate bowls). Sift the flour, cacao powder, baking powder, bicarbonate of soda/baking soda and salt through the sieve/strainer, using a whisk to help it through. Use a spatula to incorporate all the ingredients into a smooth batter, adding soy milk to reach the necessary consistency – it should not slide down the spoon. If it does, chill the batter in the fridge for 10 minutes before continuing.

Drop the batter onto the lined baking sheet using a tablespoon, placing the drops 1 cm/⅜ in. apart. Bake in the preheated oven for 12–14 minutes. The dough is dark to start with, so it's easy to burn the cookies. You want them still soft to the touch when they are out of the oven, so check for doneness after 12 minutes, and bake them for no longer than 14 minutes! The baking time is essential; 1 minute too long and they will not stay soft and gooey.

Slide the parchment paper with the cookies onto the kitchen counter or onto a cold tray and let cool. Store in a cookie jar for a week or so.

CHICKPEA & CHOCOLATE CHIP COOKIES

These chewy and chocolatey cookies are a great dessert to have on-hand. They get their great texture from coconut oil, have just the right amount of sweetness, and use protein-rich chickpea/gram flour.

2 tablespoons ground chia seeds
120 ml/½ cup gently melted coconut oil
100 g/½ cup coconut sugar or soft light brown sugar
1 teaspoon vanilla extract
185 g/1½ cups chickpea/ gram flour
1 teaspoon baking powder
¼ teaspoon salt
50 g/⅓ cup dark/ bittersweet vegan chocolate chips or roughly chopped chocolate
flaky sea salt, for sprinkling on top (optional)

baking sheet, lined with parchment paper

MAKES ABOUT 12

Combine the ground chia seeds with 6 tablespoons of water in a large bowl and whisk to combine; this should form a gel-like consistency. Add the melted coconut oil to the bowl with the chia seeds, along with the sugar and vanilla. Whisk with a hand-held electric whisk until well combined.

In a separate medium bowl, combine the chickpea/gram flour, baking powder and salt. Add these dry ingredients to the wet ingredients and mix to combine everything using a rubber spatula. (Your cookie batter will be slightly wetter than a typical cookie batter, but don't worry.) Stir in the chocolate chips until evenly dispersed. Place the batter in the fridge to firm up for 30–60 minutes.

Preheat the oven to 180°C (350°F) Gas 4.

Scoop the chilled mixture into ping pong-sized balls, using a spoon, and space evenly apart on the prepared baking sheet. Press each cookie gently using a piece of parchment paper and your hand to flatten them slightly. Sprinkle each cookie with a small pinch of sea salt (if using).

Bake in the preheated oven for 11–12 minutes (if they look a little underdone, that's okay). Remove from the oven and leave to cool on the baking sheet for 5–10 minutes before transferring to a wire rack to cool fully. Store in an airtight container at room temperature for up to 5 days.

AQUAFABA PAVLOVA WITH FRESH FRUIT

Aquafaba is the water that chickpeas are cooked in. This ingredient amazingly acts like egg whites in many dishes, making it a great plant-based substitution in a pavlova. This recipe can be a bit of a diva – whipping times can vary and the aquafaba has to be properly chilled. However, the prep is pretty easy if you have all your ducks in a row. Your end result should have a crispy outer shell with a slightly hollow, soft, almost marshmallowy inside. Don't worry if your pavlova deflates a little after cooking, you're going to top it with cream and fresh fruit anyway.

150 g/¾ cup caster/
    superfine sugar
2 tablespoons arrowroot
    powder or cornflour/
    cornstarch
a pinch of salt
liquid from a 400-g/14-oz.
    can no-added salt (low
    sodium) organic
    chickpeas, chilled in the
    fridge overnight
1 teaspoon apple cider
    vinegar
1 teaspoon vanilla extract

TO SERVE
whipped cream
220 g/1½ cups fresh fruit
    (such as berries, sliced
    peaches, figs or mangoes)
icing/confectioners' sugar
    for dusting (optional)

*large baking sheet, lined with
    parchment paper*

SERVES 6-8

Preheat the oven to 150°C (300°F) Gas 2.

Place a large mixing bowl in the freezer for a few minutes to make it extra cold. In another bowl, combine the sugar, arrowroot (or cornflour/cornstarch) and salt.

In the large chilled bowl, put the chilled aquafaba liquid (straight out of the fridge) and vinegar and beat with a hand-held electric whisk or in a stand mixer at a medium speed for about 2–4 minutes, until soft peaks begin to form, scraping down the sides of the bowl once or twice. While still mixing, start adding the sugar mixture, one spoonful at a time. When all the sugar has been added, beat for about 3–6 minutes until stiff, glossy peaks form. You should be able to turn the bowl upside down without the mixture moving at the end of whipping. Add the vanilla extract and beat for another 10 seconds.

Tip the mixture onto the prepared baking sheet and form into a 20-cm/8-in. wide circle using a rubber spatula. Leave space around the edges, as it will spread a bit.

Put in the oven and immediately lower the temperature to 120°C (250°F) Gas ½. Bake for 1½–2 hours until the outer shell is hardened when you tap it. Turn off the heat and allow the pavlova to cool completely inside the closed oven. When ready, top with whipped cream, fruit and sugar and serve immediately.

CACAO & RUM HUMMUS DESSERT WITH WHIPPED CHICKPEA CREAM

Since plain cooked chickpeas have a similar texture and taste to cooked chestnuts (which are great in desserts when in season), why not use chickpeas instead, and have this treat all year round! Cacao powder, as well as vanilla and cinnamon, will camouflage the mild beany taste of the chickpeas. And the whipped cream – you won't believe the amazing texture and taste you will get just by whipping chickpea cooking liquid!

CACAO HUMMUS
320 g/2¼ cups cooked
  chickpeas, plus 60 ml/
  ¼ cup chickpea cooking
  liquid, or more if needed
3–4 tablespoons dark agave
  syrup or maple syrup
3–4 tablespoons raw cacao
  powder
1 tablespoon rum (optional)
¼ teaspoon bourbon vanilla
  powder or ½ teaspoon
  pure vanilla extract
¼ teaspoon ground
  cinnamon
a pinch of salt

WHIPPED CREAM
120 ml/½ cup chickpea
  cooking liquid, well
  chilled
¼ teaspoon bourbon vanilla
  powder
1 tablespoon maple sugar,
  or other sugar
shaved dark/bittersweet
  chocolate or cacao
  powder, to decorate

SERVES 2

For the cacao hummus, blend all the ingredients into a creamy hummus, starting with 3 tablespoons of syrup and 3 tablespoons of cacao powder and adding cooking liquid as required to reach the desired consistency. Bear in mind that the pudding will thicken with time, so if you're not serving it right away, make it a touch softer. Taste and see if you need to add more cacao or syrup, or both.

For the whipped cream, whisk the chilled chickpea liquid with an electric hand mixer until soft peaks are formed. Add the vanilla and sugar and whisk to form semi-firm peaks. Use immediately or whisk again briefly before using (some liquid might separate, if not used straight away).

Serve the whipped cream on top of the pudding and decorate with shavings of dark/bittersweet chocolate or sift some cacao powder on top.

CAROB HUMMUS MOUSSE

Instead of cacao, why not use another superfood once in a while – the aromatic carob, for example. It's sweet-tasting, nutritious and pairs up well with cacao butter and whipped chickpea cream.

MOUSSE
320 g/2¼ cups cooked chickpeas (see page 4), plus 240 ml/1 cup chickpea cooking liquid
20 g/2 tablespoons cacao butter
2 tablespoons fine carob powder
3 tablespoons maple or agave syrup
¼ teaspoon bourbon vanilla sugar
2 tablespoons fresh raspberries, to serve

GARNISH
2 teaspoons maple syrup
1 teaspoon maple sugar (used to bind ingredients)
½ teaspoon ground cinnamon
¼ teaspoon allspice
¼ teaspoon bourbon vanilla sugar

baking sheet lined with parchment paper

SERVES 2

For the mousse, first whip the chickpea liquid with a stand mixer in a bigger bowl, for about 4 minutes or until soft peaks start forming. If done correctly, it should triple in size.

In a double boiler, melt the cacao butter. Set aside half the chickpeas for the garnish. Place the other half of the chickpeas, melted cacao butter, carob powder, syrup, vanilla sugar and whipped chickpea cream in a blender and start blending, scraping down the ingredients from the side of the bowl. Blend for 1 minute, or until velvety. Cover and refrigerate for at least 3 hours.

For the garnish, preheat the oven to 220°C (425°F) Gas 7.

Place the reserved chickpeas for the garnish on the lined baking sheet. Bake in the preheated oven for 25 minutes or until golden and slightly crunchy. Immediately after baking, place them into a bowl and add the remaining garnish ingredients. Mix thoroughly. Use the chickpeas warm as a garnish for this dessert, or store for later (although, they are best when freshly made). If using later, put back into the hot oven for about 5 minutes.

Divide the chilled mousse into 2 dessert glasses, then add the garnish and raspberries. Serve immediately.

CHOCOLATE CHICKPEA DIP

This dip is a healthy alternative to a chocolate fondue, packed with protein and natural sugar alternatives. It goes well with a variety of sweet dippers, making it a perfect sharing dessert for gatherings and parties. This is also great for kids, or anyone with a sweet tooth — you will be surprised by how creamy this dip is!

400-g/14-oz. can salt-free chickpeas (or rinse them very well)
25 g/¼ cup raw cacao powder
60 ml/¼ cup maple syrup
60 ml/¼ cup coconut cream or coconut milk
1 teaspoon vanilla extract

SERVES 4

Drain and thoroughly rinse the canned chickpeas, then put them into a blender or food processor. Add in all the remaining ingredients and blend until creamy, scraping the side of the blender or food processor if needed.

Serve in a bowl with fruit, crackers, pancakes or biscuits/cookies to dip.

CACAO HUMMUS ICE-CREAM CUPS

Chickpeas have been used for desserts since Roman times, so it's not a new thing at all! Give this ice-cream a try – cacao hummus can be used as a base for different types of sweet treats, and it works well even for frozen desserts!

3 ripe bananas
100 g/½ cup cacao hummus (see page 132)
¼ teaspoon Bourbon vanilla powder or 1 teaspoon pure vanilla extract
2 tablespoons cacao nibs
1 teaspoon coconut oil
60 ml/¼ cup coconut milk, if necessary (for weaker blenders)

TO SERVE
maple or agave syrup
shaved coconut flakes
cacao nibs
fresh cherries

SERVES 2

Peel and chop the bananas. Freeze the pieces on a small tray placed directly in the freezer. You can do this a day ahead.

Before blending, let the bananas sit at room temperature for a couple of minutes, to soften a little. Blend all the ingredients in a high-speed blender for 1–2 minutes, scraping the ingredients down the side of the bowl. Start with low speed and increase the speed slowly.

Serve in ice-cream cups, drizzled with syrup, sprinkled with shaved coconut flakes, cacao nibs and garnished with fresh cherries. Enjoy immediately!

Note: If you own a weaker blender, let the frozen banana pieces sit at room temperature for 10 minutes or until they get somewhat softer and easier to blend. The texture of the ice-cream won't be as creamy, however.

HUMMUS & WALNUT CRÊPES

Vegan alternatives to desserts can be just as delicious and exciting. Here's a dairy-free and sugar-free dessert with the addition of hummus in place of butter and cream in the filling. These pancakes are every bit as good as the classic non-vegan version that you may have enjoyed for breakfast or dessert as a child – and much healthier, too!

CRÊPES
165 ml/¾ cup soy milk
110 ml/½ cup sparkling water or water
¼ teaspoon salt
¼ teaspoon baking powder
130 g/1 cup plain/all-purpose or spelt flour
coconut oil, for frying

FILLING
140 g/1 cup walnuts
160 g/1¼ cups cooked chickpeas (see page 4)
160 g/16 stoned/pitted dates
½ teaspoon vanilla extract
240 ml/1 cup plant-based milk, warmed

TO SERVE
maple syrup (or other syrup)
sliced strawberries (or other berries)
vegan vanilla ice cream (optional)

SERVES 4

For the crêpes, combine the soy milk and water. Do not substitute soy milk with other plant-based milks or the crêpes will be sticky and fall apart. Add the salt and baking powder. Slowly add the flour, whisking vigorously. The batter should be thicker than a usual egg pancake batter. Let sit for 15 minutes, or longer.

Heat a cast-iron frying pan/skillet and brush with coconut oil before each new crêpe. Pour a small ladleful of the batter into the pan and spread it evenly, approximately 20 cm/8 in. in diameter. Once the edges start getting golden brown, turn the crêpe over and fry for another minute.

For the filling, preheat the oven to 180°C (360°F) Gas 4.

Spread the walnuts onto a baking sheet and dry-roast for 8–10 minutes until golden and fragrant (be careful, walnuts burn easily). Stir once during baking. Grind the roasted walnuts into a fine flour. This step can be done well in advance. Set aside 2 tablespoons to serve.

Blend the chickpeas with the dates, vanilla and milk until smooth; about 1 minute. Stir in the ground walnuts.

Place 1 full tablespoon of filling on the bottom half of each pancake, spread evenly and fold with the upper half. Fold once again to get a triangle. Some of the filling should stick out a little – this makes them very appetising.

Just before serving, drizzle with maple syrup and sprinkle the reserved ground walnuts on top. Decorate with strawberries or other berries and serve with ice cream, if you like.

INDEX

RECIPE CREDITS

Dunja Gulin
Baked chickpea pancake
Cacao & rum hummus dessert with chickpea cream
Cacao hummus ice-cream cups
Carob hummus mousse
Chickpea flour & harissa patties
Chickpea fudge cookies
Creamy hummus
Falafel coconut curry
Fennel & lemon scented falafel pockets
Heat & eat falafel casserole
Hummus & walnut crepes
Luscious undone falafel salad
Perfectly charred falafel burgers
Purple beetroot hummus
Vegan devilled 'eggs'

Ghillie Başan
Chickpea & spinach tagine with yogurt
Chickpea & vegetable soup with feta
Chickpea salad with onions & paprika
Hot hummus with pine nuts & chilli butter
Spicy carrot & chickpea tagine with turmeric & coriander
Spicy chickpeas & onions with yogurt & pitta bread

Claire Power
Chickpea nuggets
Chickpea 'omelettes'
Chickpea ratatouille stew
Chickpea satay curry
Chocolate chickpea dip
Socca crackers

Nicola Graimes
Char-grilled halloumi, courgette & chickpea salad
Chickpea & spiced cauliflower salad with tamarind dressing
Chickpea, squash & spinach salad with dukkah
Honey-roasted carrots & chickpeas with citrus cream

Vicky Jones
Chickpea, egg & potato salad
Sicilian chickpea fritters
Spiced chickpea & spinach pasties
Syrian aubergine & chickpea ragout

Leah Vanderveldt
Aquafaba pavlova with fresh fruit
Chickpea 'tikka' masala
Chickpea & chocolate chip cookies
Chickpea socca pancakes with mushrooms & thyme

Nitisha Patel
Chickpea, kale & coconut curry
Dhokla muffins
Spiced lentil & chickpea burgers

Jenny Tschiesche
Chickpea & pepper curry bake
Cumin-roasted chickpeas
Vegan baked chickpea fajitas

Chloe Coker and Jane Montgomery
Chickpea & vegetable stew
Herby chickpea pancakes with halloumi & roasted corn & red pepper salsa

Ross Dobson
Chickpea, tomato & green bean minestrone soup
Pasta e fagioli

Jenny Linford
Chickpea & mushroom freekah pilaff
Chickpea, chard & potato stew

Ursula Ferrigno
Fried chickpeas with herbs
Leek & chickpeas with mustard dressing

Laura Washburn
Avocado & chickpea wraps
Chickpea bites

Sarah Wilkinson
Moroccan chickpea pumpkin stew
Quinoa tabbouleh with spinach falafel

Jordan Bourke
Pan-fried chickpea fritters

Amy Ruth Finegold
Linseed-speckled hummus with kale crisps

Mat Follas
Broad bean hummus

Liz Franklin
Spiced chickpea, tomato & almond curry

Jackie Kearney
Chickpea 'chuna' quesadillas with jimaca slaw

Theo A. Michaels
Chana saag paneer

Hannah Miles
Moroccan chickpea soup with falafel & harissa pockets

Milli Taylor
Beetroot, dill & goat's cheese cups

Jenna Zoe
Party tartlets with hummus

PICTURE CREDITS

Tim Atkins
Pages 29, 64, 66–67, 80, 93, 106

Jan Baldwin
Pages 17, 72

Peter Cassidy
Pages 63, 79

Richard Jung
Pages 60, 77, 118, 135

Mowie Kay
Front cover, pages 5, 9–11, 14, 22, 26, 97, 124–126, 133–134, 138, 141

Adrian Lawrence
Pages 75, 89, 117

David Munns
Page 50

Steve Painter
Pages 13, 53, 56, 59, 98, 105, 110, 122

William Reavell
Pages 33, 41, 46–49, 57, 62, 78, 111-113 , 121

Matt Russell
Pages 54–55, 76, 83-87

Toby Scott
Page 45

Ian Wallace
Page 100

Kate Whitaker
Pages 23, 34, 51, 82, 92, 136

Clare Winfield
Pages 5, 8, 12, 18-21, 25, 30, 35–38, 42–43, 65, 68, 71, 88, 90, 94, 109, 114, 129–130, 137